Sweet Peas for Summer

Sweet Peas for Summer

HOW TO CREATE A GARDEN IN A YEAR

LAETITIA MAKLOUF

WITH A FOREWORD BY ALAN TITCHMARSH

PHOTOGRAPHY BY JILL MEAD

BLOOMSBURY

LONDON · BERLIN · NEW YORK · SYDNEY

FOR THE HUNK

FIRST PUBLISHED IN GREAT BRITAIN 2012

TEXT © 2012 BY LAETITIA MAKLOUF
FOREWORD © 2012 BY ALAN TITCHMARSH
ILLUSTRATIONS © 2012 BY GEORGIA VAUX
PHOTOGRAPHY © 2012 BY JILL MEAD
ADDITIONAL PHOTOGRAPHY BY LAETITIA MAKLOUF

THE MORAL RIGHT OF THE AUTHOR HAS BEEN ASSERTED

BLOOMSBURY PUBLISHING PLC,
50 BEDFORD SQUARE, LONDON WC1B 3DP

BLOOMSBURY PUBLISHING, LONDON,
BERLIN, NEW YORK AND SYDNEY

A CIP CATALOGUE RECORD FOR THIS BOOK IS
AVAILABLE FROM THE BRITISH LIBRARY

ISBN 978 1 4088 1486 4

10 9 8 7 6 5 4 3 2 1

PHOTOGRAPHY: JILL MEAD
DESIGN AND ILLUSTRATION: GEORGIA VAUX
INDEX: HILARY BIRD

PRINTED AND BOUND IN CHINA

WWW.BLOOMSBURY.COM/LAETITIAMAKLOUF
WWW.LAETITIAMAKLOUF.COM

Spring

Summer

Autumn

Winter

Foreword by Alan Titchmarsh

You know that feeling? The one where you finally have a patch of land that you can call your own and you just want to see it brimming with flowers, a-flutter with butterflies and bees, and filled with the scent of sweet peas and roses, rosemary and thyme? But quickly? Well, Laetitia Maklouf knows it well, and her first-hand experience of turning a tired old lump of ground behind her London house into a romantic oasis within twelve months is a beguiling introduction to the world of gardening.

Here there are no instructions on hard landscaping, no designs for elaborate water features or expensive patios, no complicated formal plans. No, this is a book that allows you to start growing things straight away, sowing seeds in a patch of cleared earth and establishing border plants; all the fancy stuff can come later.

Of course, planning is important, but so too is striking while the iron is hot and creating something you love. All too often that initial feeling of excitement can be lost in a welter of technical detail. Not in Laetitia's garden. With a few old fruit trees and a patch of rough grass as her starter kit, she shows you just what she managed to achieve in that first year. Her enthusiasm is infectious and her words persuasive, and the pictures that accompany them are the stuff of reality.

In a world where it is easy to be overwhelmed at the prospect of gardening from scratch, this is a refreshing book that will inspire anyone who wants to fill their heart and mind with that elusive optimism that can only come as a result of making things grow.

A BEGINNING

In February last year I finally stepped out of the back door of our new house and into my first garden. This was the sweet culmination of months of searching, but more importantly, it represented the beginning of a whole new set of horticultural possibilities for me; all the gardening I had done before had been confined to the flat I was living in, its balcony and tiny back yard, where I happily pottered about with my dog, Mr Pug, and hundreds of plants in pots.

My love for growing stuff had blossomed from humble beginnings: an over-flowing cupboard, emptied in a fit of spring-cleaning pique, had yielded the remnants of a three-year-old Christmas stocking, cast aside in favour of I don't know what ... better presents? Breakfast perhaps? Inside was a walnut, a shrunken, wizened tangerine, and a packet of sweet pea seeds. I planted them, they sprouted, and my life was never the same again. Course after horticultural course followed, and I learned very quickly that you didn't have to have a garden in order to surround yourself with greenery. I got totally absorbed in my plants, and apart from the fact that I didn't yet have a proper garden to call my own, my life was utterly complete.

Then one day a dark, handsome Hunk appeared, followed closely by a small but life-changing bundle of baby whom we named Jemima Velvet, and very soon we realised we needed somewhere with more space. At last I would have the opportunity to create a garden for us.

The new space was larger than the average London garden and oddly shaped; a long, narrow strip with two apple trees in it, which I named 'The Apple Garden', and then another, bigger bit at the end ('The Garden Proper'), much of which was invisible from the house. There were more trees in this second part of the garden – another apple, a pear and two plums, and in the corner next to the shed, along with a large amount of junk and building materials, was a huge sycamore tree, full of birds. The previous owner had obviously done some gardening, as there was a shed (complete with holes in the roof) and quite a few useful tools left behind, but apart from a smattering of forget-me-nots, the whole of the garden was covered with grass.

One freezing, bleak February day I stood out there with a mug of tea, and made myself a promise: I would have this garden not just planted, but up and blooming and full of bees and butterflies by summertime. I was ready for the hard graft, but there had to be a summer (not next summer but *this* summer) of picnics and flower-picking at the end of it. This book is the story of that year: the hard graft and dirty hands, the flower-filled summer and autumn, the plants and their freezing first winter, and the successes and failures all the way through. It is also a practical guide for those wishing to create a garden from scratch.

The emphasis here is less on getting the builders in, and more about working with what's already there to achieve a plant-filled Eden in a relatively short timescale and without breaking the bank. True, you may eventually want to build gazebos and terraces, and have fountains and sunken gardens galore, but if you use plants as a starting point, you can enjoy your garden now and do the expensive stuff later without the years slipping by while you wait for the perfect moment.

Those who dream of a new garden usually fall into one of two camps: either the garden is a complete wasteland (empty or filled with rubbish); or it is an existing garden, inherited from previous owners and, for whatever reason, you don't love it. If you've moved into an existing garden, it's best (if you can bear to wait) to live with it for a year and get to know the plants. I promise you will find treasure that you will want to keep. Make notes and take photographs of what you love as the year progresses. Tie ribbons or labels around everything that excites you (plants change so much with the seasons, so this is really important). Pay particular attention to shrubs and trees, but also try to do this with herbaceous plants (herbaceous plants are the ones that disappear underground over winter). Consult reference books and the internet, and as soon as you have a vague idea of the plants in your space and the ones you want to keep, you can get on and create the garden of your dreams, saving quite a bit of money in the process. Once you have spent some time with your garden, or if you are one of those people who have moved into a space with no redeeming plants, then it's time for some action (see How to create a garden in ten easy steps on page 12).

This ten-step plan will help you make a gorgeous garden as quickly as possible and without it becoming overwhelming. Growing a garden is challenging, but it's not rocket science. The big message here is that it's possible to do most, if not all of this stuff yourself and without spending lots of money.

I'll take you through each season, month by month, chronicling the progress of my garden, and suggesting how you can create your own 'Virgin Garden' from scratch. I have also included short 'recipes' for fun, easy projects to do each month, which, unless otherwise stated, are possible even if you don't yet have a garden. Regard them as little tasters, which I hope will ease you into the pleasurable activity of gardening, without too much fuss, huff or puff. So if you've chosen to wait and ponder a while longer, you can still indulge in a bit of clandestine 'unofficial' gardening on the side.

This book begins at the start of the gardening year in spring. You can of course start planning and preparing your new garden much earlier than this, but the reality is that most of us like to stay cosily indoors when it's chilly. The good news, though, is that it's perfectly possible to plan, prepare and plant a new garden in spring and have a flower-filled paradise by summer – you are, after all, simply following nature's way of doing things.

HOW TO CREATE A GARDEN IN TEN EASY STEPS

You don't have to have a degree in garden design or be hugely organised to create something beautiful and floriferous from scratch in one year, as long as you get a wriggle on. Here's my guide to making your garden in ten steps. Of course, if you're properly organised, you can get most of this done before Christmas, and if that's the case, then I utterly salute you, but if you're an ordinary mortal, you'll have been too busy eating mince pies with your friends and family to be outside doing hard labour for any meaningful amount of time. And, for this reason, my guide to getting your garden under way begins in March.

STEP 1 **Clear your site**

It's vitally important to have company when you're doing this; old sofas are heavy, bits of broken glass are dangerous, and clearing a jungle of weeds is hard work, but it is rewarding and lovely when it's done, so rope some helpers in with the promise of great food and drink, and make a weekend of it. Make sure you save any 'found objects', like old tools, or pretty pieces of china; old tools are often in good order after a bit of a clean. And leave any established plants, especially trees, and clear as many weeds as possible. Even in the depths of winter it's possible to establish whether you have a problem with perennial weeds. The biggest culprits are bindweed and couch-grass. You can of course get rid of them by using chemicals, and this is something to consider seriously if the problem is a big one, but hand-weeding, slowly, steadily and thoroughly is the best way to keep them under control, and you will get to know your garden intimately in the process.

STEP 2 **Get to know your soil**

Go to one of those big garden centres and buy a soil testing kit. Use the test tubes, powders and tiny spoons to find out the pH of your soil, and take a look at the table opposite to establish the condition of your garden's soil and how to improve what you've got. This knowledge is vital when it comes to choosing your plants; all plant encyclopedias give details of the sort of conditions that each plant likes, so you'll be able to choose plants for your garden accordingly.

TYPE	DESCRIPTION	IMPROVEMENTS
SANDY	Large particles with big gaps between them. Light, easy to work. Very fast draining. Poor fertility, as nutrients are washed away.	Add organic matter every year. Mulch (see page 33) for water conservation. Feed plants.
CLAY	Tiny particles which cake together. Heavy in winter, rock hard in summer. Slow draining. Rich in nutrients.	Add organic matter every year. Add sand or grit to break it up.
LOAM	Mixture of clay and sand. Perfect drainage. Good fertility.	Add organic matter every few years.
CHALKY	Crumbly soil with chalky bits. Often shallow and low in nutrients. Fast drainage.	Add organic matter whenever possible. Mulch for water conservation. Feed plants.
CITY SOIL	Often exhausted, low in nutrients. Either dusty or compacted.	Add organic matter regularly. Feed plants. Add sand, grit or soil-improver.

STEP 3 **Begin designing your space**

This is a slow process and you should take your time with it, because making a garden requires money and effort – you don't want to go wasting either of those. Remember that this is about how you'll use your garden, not whether you'll have pink or blue delphiniums (that comes later). Here's how to do it …

Make a list of your dreams and desires. Borrow or buy some garden magazines and rip out pictures of scenes or flowers that you love. Pay particular attention to pictures of gardens in winter, which will help you to learn the importance of structure in your space. If you can spare the time, visit some great gardens – winter is the best time to go because there is no froth to distract you and you get to see structure (evergreen topiary, hedging, shrubbery and effective hard landscaping and garden furniture) in all its glory. This is what gardeners refer to as 'bones'. Go absolutely wild and don't even think about money or time or space considerations when you make your list.

Write a list of your practical needs. What do you need out of your garden? Somewhere to sit? Somewhere to have cocktails? A place for a climbing frame? You'll be surprised how many of your practical needs overlap with your dreams and desires, and that's a good thing because …

Now compromise. Only you know what's possible for you. Your decisions and compromises will depend on your budget and the amount of space you have, so the next trick is to concentrate on three or four of your top priorities. For me this meant having a space to play (a lawn), a space to eat and drink outside (a paved area) and as big a planting area as possible to feed my gardening addiction. I also needed space for a compost heap and a place to keep tools, pots and a lawnmower.

When you've decided on your priorities and pin-pointed the areas you need in your garden, it's time to establish where to put them. It's essential to get outside for this step, so wrap up warm and look at your space with new eyes. The possibilities will soon become evident as long as you give yourself time to mull them over. Think about how you want your space to work for you. Imagine it as a blank slate, and that there are no limitations. Go out there at different times of the day, and make a mental note of where the sun is in the morning and evening, and the shadows cast by any walls or existing trees or shrubs. If you think that the ultimate seating area would be perfect slap bang in the middle of an existing flowerbed, then get in there with a chair and sit down. It's essential that you spend time doing this, because you'll change your mind again and again. These are important decisions and you may be spending money getting these areas sorted, so consider:

Aspect. You want to drink your cocktails in the apricot glow of the evening sun, not shivering in the shade.

Shelter. Seating areas need to be out of the wind. If your perfect site is very exposed, you'll need to think about building (or better still, growing) a windbreak (see Planting a hedge on page 191).

Ease of use. If your eating area is too far from your kitchen you may never use it ... and that would be a shame.

And that's it. Once you've decided roughly how you want to live in your garden, you're ready to put it all down on paper. If you think you're going to need building work, then do your design straight away and get people in to quote for the work.

STEP 4   **Make a scale plan**
This is easy in a small space that has a few straight lines; it's more difficult if your garden is a weird shape. All you need is a really long tape-measure, a pencil and paper and a clip-board (yes, you read that right). Try to get help for this – it's much quicker with two people.

First, do a rough bird's-eye view sketch of the garden on your paper. It is impossible for this to be accurate so don't even try – just make sure everything is there. Mark the perimeter down, along with any existing buildings and trees. Now start with the first perimeter length and measure it. Note this measurement down on the plan and keep going until you have measurements for the whole thing, including whichever wall of your house backs on to the space.

Next, you need to start getting the trees and any freestanding buildings on to your plan. To do this, take two or three fixed points at your perimeter and measure from each one to the object. This takes some time but remember, unless you're planning something deeply intricate, it doesn't have to be perfect. This plan is purely an aid for you when you come to put your design down on paper. It will help you to work out how many plants you need to fill your flowerbeds. (Although you could skip this and just do it by eye … there's nothing wrong with that.)

Once you've got all your measurements, drawing a scale plan requires nothing more than graph paper, some tracing paper and a ruler (you can buy rulers that translate into different scales – each centimetre represents half a metre, for example). Decide on your scale and draw up your plan. Of course, this is the low-tech option; there are endless computer-aided design programs that will do the same thing, but they're only necessary if you're planning on doing this for a living.

STEP 5 **Put your design on paper**

Photocopy your scale plan at least a dozen times and start drawing your garden. Each drawing will get you a step closer to your final design. Try to make each drawing as different as possible from the previous one, so that a very geometric garden, with lots of straight lines, becomes a really sinuous one that's all curves. This process will help you to see what the options are, and you'll instinctively know which design is right for you.

Bear in mind that you'll need access to your flowerbeds in order to maintain them. If you're planning a huge, deep border, be aware that you'll want to get to the back of it. The optimum width for easy access without stepping into a bed is however far you can reach (around 60cm), which would give you a perfectly practical, but rather mean-looking flowerbed. In practice, and however small your garden, think about having beds double this size; it's a strange thing, but the more generous you are with your planting, the bigger your space will feel. It's easy to step into your flowerbeds once you get acquainted with the planting but if they are really wide, then it might be worth putting a few stepping-stones down to help you.

Where possible, work what's already there into your design. It's a real shame to cut down established trees, so consider pruning them creatively if you feel they are taking up too much space.

It's a good idea to 'fool' the eye in a garden and create surprises, particularly in small spaces. It can initially seem like madness to cut a garden in half by placing a hedge in the middle of it, but in practice this serves to make the garden feel bigger because of the element of surprise. Be as witty and playful as possible and create interesting viewpoints and secret spaces – being in a garden can be an adventure.

I often find it useful to mark out a grid in square metres on a piece of graph paper and lay it under my plan. With one square placed centrally at a certain point, like a door or a window, the grid helps to establish important viewpoints in the garden and, if you design around them, everything will instantly feel 'right', rather than awkward. I also use this to help me lay out special plants (see How to create a planting plan on page 20).

The important thing here is not to spend the whole of spring indoors with a pencil and paper – decide on a design (even if you have to toss a coin) and get the thing marked out and dug so you can spend the summer in your gorgeous garden.

STEP 6 **Mark out the garden**

Once it's all down on paper you'll want to get going. Use string and stakes to mark out the beds, always referring to your master plan. This is a really important step because seeing your design marked out will show up any mistakes you may have made. It is also an essential element of digging your beds, as you'll be using your markers to guide your spade correctly. Simply go outside with your master plan and tape-measure, and 'draw' the design on the ground using string stretched taut between short bamboo canes (I cut mine into 50cm lengths using secateurs). If you're going for curves, then use a long length of hosepipe to mark out a clean curve. You can then either peg it down to make sure it doesn't move or use outdoor marker spray-paint to trace the line. Make sure you're happy with the size of things, and that the areas are generous enough.

Of course, it's not essential to have a plan at all. If you feel happy marking out using your instinct and good judgement, then definitely go for it. This obviously works best with curvy, irregular shaped areas, because there's no 'right or wrong'. Straight edges are less forgiving, but can still be fudged to a certain extent.

STEP 7 **Dig your beds**

Once you've decided on your plan and marked it out, recruit some friends and family to help dig your beds (bribe them with really good sandwiches). You'd be surprised how much you can get done under this 'many hands make light work' system. Teach them how to single dig your beds (see opposite) and watch your garden take shape before your very eyes.

FIRST TRENCH	START HERE
SECOND TRENCH	
THIRD TRENCH	
AND SO ON	
UNTIL	
YOU	
GET	
TO	
THE	
LAST TRENCH	EARTH FROM FIRST TRENCH GOES HERE

Single digging couldn't be simpler. Once you've marked out the bed, start at one end and dig a trench all the way across to the depth of your spade (the metal bit) and put the earth you've dug out into a wheelbarrow or container.

Add to the bottom of the trench some soil-improver or well-rotted manure, which you can buy in bags or beg from a reputable local stable. Make absolutely sure any manure is well-rotted. This process kills any weed seeds and ensures that the roots of your plants won't get 'burned' by any urine, which is too concentrated for plants in its fresh state. The best way to tell if manure has been rotted properly is to smell it – it should no longer smell of horse poo (if it pongs, then it needs to rot a while longer).

Now shuffle backwards and dig an identical trench right alongside the first one, putting all the earth from this trench on top of the manure in the first trench, and breaking up any large clods while you're at it. Keep repeating this process until you get to the end of the bed. When you've dug the last trench and added manure, fill it up with the earth in the wheelbarrow from the first trench. Voila – you have a wonderful manure-filled 'sandwich'. It will be raised up slightly, because of all the air and manure you've put in, and it will look clean and comfy and ready for some plants (which it is).

It goes without saying that you should pull out weeds and big stones as you go. If you're digging flowerbeds out of an area of turf, you'll need to remove this first, by cutting small squares out with the edge of your spade and sliding your spade underneath to dislodge them. You can compost these turf squares by laying them upside down in a pile. Eventually, you'll be left with lovely compost, so don't throw it away. Oh, and one more thing: digging a flowerbed like this burns more calories than going for a serious run, so definitely have some chocolate.

STEP 8 **Create a planting plan**

Now for the fun bit. Planting plans need a bit of know-how but are much easier than many people think. All you need is a plant encyclopedia and a knowledge of your own whims and desires. Go back to the garden magazines and start looking at plants. Don't worry about individual plants yet, just notice textures, colours and shapes that give you goosebumps. Create one of those 'moodboards' or a scrapbook if you like – it's great to have something that reminds you of your dream, and it's really useful when you come to choose plants for your garden.

Make a lust list of plants you utterly love and start with this – you'll be surprised how easy it is to produce a planting scheme from scratch (see page 20). However, I do understand that umming and ahhing over different plants and making sure there's something of interest in a particular space all year round is not everyone's idea of fun. So, with that in mind, I've created some very simple template planting plans (see page 270) with associated plant lists that you can reduce or expand to suit your new borders.

STEP 9 **Order your plants**

The fun part. This hardly needs explaining – we all know how to shop. The important thing here is to get a move on. You don't want all the organised folks getting those plants before you do, so put your order in as soon as possible – you'll be glad you did, because once you have a virgin garden ready to plant, you'll be gagging to get going. In an ideal world, one stockist will have everything you need, but in reality you'll probably have to shop around a bit if you're craving certain cultivars or colours. I have listed my favourite plant websites on page 280.

STEP 10 **Plant your garden**

Once your order has arrived, place everything in its allotted space and plant it well (see page 30). Now it's time to sit back and wait for the magic to happen: watch your garden grow.

HOW TO CREATE A PLANTING PLAN

This is, honestly, no big deal– you just need a knowledge of what you love and a willingness to compromise. Remember that the point of this is not to create a pretty picture, but to give yourself a more accurate shopping list so you don't waste money and time on plants you don't need or have room for. Your planting plan will be a scale drawing of your plot with lots of blobs and writing on it denoting which plant goes where.

To create a planting plan you need three things:

1   An understanding of your garden's constraints – soil type, aspect, sun/shade.
2   A plant encyclopedia divided into colour sections or a book of plants, or a self-collated list of plants you love (your lust list), researched and refined according to your site's constraints.
3   Your scale plan (see step 4 on page 14), photocopied several times on thin paper or tracing paper and laid over your grid if you are using one, and a pencil.

There are two ways to get started with a planting plan. I like to dream up a patchwork of different shapes and heights first, and then decide which plants to use afterwards. To do this, think about how you want your flowerbed to look (formal, sprawling, decadent), and draw circles on your plan denoting the trees and shrubs that will form its backbone. Then use an encylopedia and my list below to find plants to fit your vision. The other way is to choose specific plants first and place them on the plan, again using my list below to help you. You'll probably end up doing a bit of both, particularly if you have existing shrubs or trees to work around. Have a look at the planting plan templates on pages 270–3 for inspiration.

Trees

If you don't have trees in your space, then this is the place to start – every garden, even very small ones, should have a tree. Your encyclopedia will give you a wealth of choices in the 'small', 'medium' and 'large' categories. Where you place trees will be central to how your garden grows, as they cast shade, which is often a good thing because there are hundreds of shade-loving beauties you can plant underneath. Mark your tree as a big circle with a dotted line to denote its canopy.

Evergreen shrubs

Next, you need to put in structure, and that means evergreen shrubs. You want enough of these in your garden to hold it all together. Evergreens can be dense bushes, looser structures, or column-like shapes. For a simple and cohesive look, choose one plant that you love, and repeat it several times. This will suit most people. The other way to go (and only do this if you are a plant nut) is for each of your shrubs to be different and you can then pull the look together by repeating perennials and bulbs. Find out the eventual spread of your plant and draw it on your plan as a circle, coloured in, and to scale. I almost always use a grid system to help ensure plants work within the garden's different viewpoints (see page 16).

Deciduous shrubs

Remember that these lose their leaves over the winter, so will need to be next to something that doesn't (unless of course you love the naked look). Put them in, again as circles, marking their eventual spread, but don't colour them in this time.

Climbers

Have you got walls and fences that need clothes? Climbers are brilliant for bringing drama and colour and scent into a garden whilst taking up hardly any ground area. Choose your favourites and mark them in by using a small 'v' (obviously at the base of walls or fences). Most climbers require some sort of frame to climb up, so aim to get your trellis up, or your wires erected before you plant the garden (see page 33).

Perennials

If you want a really low-maintenance garden, then forget the perennials for now and just use shrubs, but this group of plants is so utterly fabulous that most people want their favourites in situ. You should know that some of these will require staking and most will need to be cut down in the autumn or winter after they have done their delightful thing. Mark perennials down on your plan by researching their eventual spread and drawing some sort of stylised approximation of their leaf shape as seen from above, just to give you a quick indication of the kinds of textures you are introducing. Aim to group perennials in threes, fives and sevens. Be generous, but remember that eventually they will spread, so don't go overboard or you'll be having to take plants out and give them away three years later. Be aware that most perennials die down in winter so make sure there is something nearby (evergreen) to gladden the heart during the cold months.

Annuals and bedding

I don't put these on the plan as I like to determine how much I need after planting the other plants, but if you do want to draw them in, it's usually done by drawing what look like elongated ovals and fat snakes, to show a sinuous 'drift' of flowering plants.

Bulbs

Again, I like to order bulbs and put them in by eye, but there's nothing to stop you putting them on the plan, marking each one with a simple cross.

Ground-cover

This is not the same as 'gap-fillers' which are the bedding plants or annuals that you'll use to get things looking floriferous in the first year. Ground-cover plants are specifically evergreen and low-growing. Good books usually have entire sections on ground-cover plants, particularly those that can withstand difficult conditions, like dry shade near to the roots of trees. The best thing about ground-cover plants, though, is that they cut out the light and therefore compete with weeds. Mark any areas for ground-cover plants with some simple shading.

Edging

It's useful to think about low-growing shrubs or perennials, which can line a path or edge of a flowerbed, as a separate group. Edging can be evergreen or perennial but is really useful as a 'containing' element to keep things looking sort of tidy.

Height

In your garden's first year, getting height will be hugely important. You can cheat by using wigwams (see A flowering inferno on page 108), but you'll also want to plant things that will eventually give height on their own, so pay particular attention to plants that shoot upwards and take up very little space outwards. For the long-term, this means evergreens, but tall perennials will be your means of instant gratification whilst you wait patiently for your evergreens to grow.

There are no rules here, just suggestions. Okay, traditionally, you'd put really big, tall things at the back of a flowerbed and place other stuff at reducing heights towards the front, but, honestly, it really is your call. Instinct will guide you when placing your plants, so I'm not going to meddle with that.

It may feel a bit overwhelming as you get further into your plan, because things start to overlap or you need plants to come up at different times or there are spaces underneath certain shrubs that need populating with plants. My advice here is to keep it as simple as possible. Don't get too hung up on having year-round abundance, just concentrate on the summer and autumn ahead of you. You can always add to your plant list in subsequent years, and as long as you have enough evergreens and bulbs, your winter and spring will be glorious.

When it comes to shrubs and perennials, stick to fully hardy plants. Unless you live somewhere with extremely clement weather, tropical plants have to be mollycoddled over the winter months, which is fine, but quite a bit of extra bother for a first-timer. Fully hardy plants are usually labelled as such or marked with three stars in an encyclopedia.

For obvious reasons try to steer clear of weird and wonderful varieties, and stick with tried and tested garden plants that are widely available. It's very easy to get caught up with wanting something rare and gorgeous, only to find that it's impossible to source, and extremely difficult to grow. There is a sort of kite mark for garden plants called the 'Award of Garden Merit', which signifies that the RHS (Royal Horticultural Society) has tested the plant and found it to be a 'good-doer'. It's a very useful way of sorting the wheat from the chaff when choosing from the myriad of plants available.

Last but not least, remember scent and use it wherever possible.

Label everything as you put it on the plan, either directly into the circle that denotes it, or with an arrow. It will probably end up decipherable only to you, but it will give you a pretty accurate shopping list, and that's all that matters. Now go forth and shop.

MY ESSENTIAL TOOLS

SPADE   For digging. Mine is a small one – it's better to have smaller tools that are easy to use than huge, unwieldy ones that are too heavy.

FORK   For digging up and dividing plants. Again, make sure the size and weight suits you.

RAKES   Use a regular one for preparing soil, and a spring-tine rake (curved and fan-shaped) for scarifying lawns and gathering fallen apples etc.

TROWELS   I have several ordinary ones, and a very long thin one (from Burgon & Ball) which is really useful for weeding.

HAND FORK   For weeding and breaking up soil. Absolutely essential for garden maintenance. Try out lots of different types in your hand and get the one that feels the most comfortable. (My one is Sophie Conran for Burgon & Ball.)

SECATEURS   You need to try lots out to find your favourites. Mine are Felco, which come in masses of different sizes and shapes, and left-handed too. Make sure you get a sharpening stone to go with them.

HAND HOE   For getting rid of weed seedlings, and another essential tool. I don't use a normal hoe at all, just this one, and I love it.

HAND SAW   For when secateurs won't cut it. Very useful.

CLIPPERS   For shaping topiary. They are just like sheep shears. If you're planning on having lots of large topiary though, think about investing in something electric.

SCISSORS   Essential, for cutting string, and flowers.

BULB PLANTERS   If you're planning a big display, this is essential and will cut down your work time considerably. I also have a long one for planting bulbs in the lawn, but that's not essential.

WHEELBARROW   Very useful, even for a small garden.

WATERING CAN At least two large ones with rose attachments (the bit that you attach to the spout to make sprinkles), and, personally, I think the cheap ones with big fat spouts are better than their posher, slimmer-spouted cousins.

TUB TRUGS I have four or five. These plastic tubs are brilliant for carrying all sorts of stuff, from clippings to potted plants.

LAWNMOWER Obviously only useful if you have a lawn. Mine is electric, and I have an extra-long extension cable.

GLOVES For light work I often just use washing-up gloves, but for the rest I have discovered Ultimax gloves, and I love them.

APRON I use a small apron (not shown below) with pockets for a phone, secateurs, string and scissors.

STRING I carry a ball of string with me absolutely everywhere.

Spring

March

Welcome to March, the beginning of everything. The party hasn't nearly started yet, but let's just say that the garden is handing out the flyers. We moved in two weeks ago, and I had already designed the garden in my head, but being here has changed all that, and now I have had time to stand and stare, I realise that the garden is much smaller than I imagined. My ambitious schemes will have to be somewhat less grand. This doesn't bother me (I've spent my whole gardening life in a space smaller than the average bathroom), and in fact, I am relieved at the sudden conclusion that things will have to be much, much simpler. I stand there in the cold and breathe a sigh of relief; bye bye sunken trampoline, so long wookiee-style tree-house ... maybe next time.

My aim is to have flowers by May, and lots of them, but also to plant the beginnings of a garden that will eventually look after itself, requiring less and less attention as it matures. Time is of the essence if I'm going to achieve this, so I'm aware that I need to get out there and measure the garden. The 'plot plan' provided by the estate agent lives up to its small print 'for reference only and not to scale'. Drawing up a scale plan of a regular-shaped garden is easy (see page 14), but for larger, weirder shapes, it's worth getting in a professional. If you have this kind of garden you need a geographical surveyor (you know, those people you see squinting into cameras on tripods at the side of the road; what a relief, finally, to know what they're doing). I call up one of these people and, within a week, I have a beautiful scale drawing, which I use to finalise the design: a sunny border along the back wall, followed by an enclosed lawn, followed by vegetable(ish) raised beds, all of which will be behind a hedge, rendering it 'secret'. The Apple Garden will just be tidied and planted up.

After lots of internet-surfing and trips to giant garden centres, as well as specialist nurseries, I've sourced my all-important shrubs: scented roses, lilac (see page 104), lavender, *Cistus* (rock roses), *Choisya* (Mexican orange blossom), *Philadelphus* (mock orange), myrtle ... the list goes on, but the common theme with all of these is that they're eventually going to take over and form the bulk of my garden, making it low-maintenance and beautiful all at once.

One day I mark out the design with string. It takes ages, and I keep tripping over the damn string (always, always use bright yellow string for marking out a garden). The next morning I realise I've been mean with the lawn, so I rearrange the string and call my friend James, who agrees to come with two friends to help dig the beds (for a price, of course). While I get busy with the planting plan, the Hunk surprises me with a homemade compost bay. I am thrilled and begin filling it straight away (see page 44). Slowly I start to plant my garden.

WHAT TO DO IN YOUR VIRGIN GARDEN THIS MONTH

PLANTING Get your plant order in or go to the garden centre and buy your plants as soon as possible. You don't have to wait until you have everything before you start planting. Once you've marked out your garden and dug any new flowerbeds, it's time to get going. Understanding when to plant requires instinct as much as knowledge, so, yes, anyone can do it. Most shrubs, bare-root trees and herbaceous plants that have been grown outside can go in the ground when it's still pretty cold, but for anything that has been nursed under glass, or displayed for sale in a sheltered environment, I would definitely wait until the frost has abated and there has been a run of milder days – the sort of days when you can go outside without hunching – that's my marker; can I expose my neck without a scarf?

While you wait for this special time, keep your potted plants close together somewhere sheltered, like next to a wall, so that they acclimatise to being properly outside. Always remember that it is better to plant or sow seeds a little late than risk losing something by being too eager.

When you plant a shrub, dig a hole twice the width and depth of the pot and put a couple of handfuls of well-rotted manure or good compost into the bottom of the planting hole. Muss this about a bit with your trowel or spade so it gets mixed up with the surrounding earth, and then carefully remove the plant from its pot. Rub the roots gently to dislodge them from the side of the moulded earth in which they've been growing, and place the whole thing into the prepared hole, so that your plant ends up in the ground at the same depth that it was in its pot. Now gently but firmly push the dug-up soil around the plant into the gaps and firm it in at the top, using your foot.

I then usually create a little 'dam' of soil around the base of the plant so that water doesn't flow away when I water it. Carefully water your new shrubs with the contents of one and-a-half to two watering cans. This will take time, as you'll have to wait for the water to soak in to the base of the plant before you can put the next lot of water in. Be patient – this is the most important part of planting. Keep watering daily for a week or so, and then every other day for another week to give your plants the very best start.

WEEDING As soon as the milder weather begins you need to begin your war on weeds. The key to this is – as with so many things – that little and often wins the day. I know very well that if we were all good at 'little and often' none of us would be fat, stressed or disorganised ... we'd live in a perfect world where everyone remembered everyone else's birthdays and we never ran out of loo paper. Although I try to tackle

weeds as and when I see them, it's more likely that I'll do one huge weeding session when I've got a spare couple of hours. As a result, my garden will never be entirely weed-free, and I'm okay with that. Do bear in mind, however, that the more weeds you remove before you plant your garden, the easier it will be to control them as time goes on, because it's much more difficult to weed around something than it is to hoe an empty bed. My favourite tools for weeding are my small hand hoe for annual weeds and a long thin trowel, which I think is supposed to be used for planting bulbs, but is brilliant for isolating and digging out perennial weeds.

COMPOSTING If you haven't already got one, this is the perfect time to start a compost heap. Either make one (see page 44) or get your council to give you one. Either way, it's worth being quite fussy about what goes on to your heap (thin layers of different material, cut up as small as possible, no cooked food and no perennial weeds … ever). It's hard to imagine, but in a year's time, if you've put the effort in to get it right, the resulting compost will be a source of immeasurable pride – so much so that you may become a compost bore. Your plants will thank you most of all, because if you feed the soil in which they grow with lovely, nutrient-rich compost, they'll repay you with gorgeousness a million times over.

MULCHING March is the traditional time to mulch your flowerbeds (a mulch is simply a thick layer of anything that will suppress weeds and/or feed the soil). Mulching with well-rotted manure or compost helps to add nutrients to the soil and suppresses weeds as it cuts out the light. Because you have incorporated organic matter into your soil already, and done lots of weeding, putting a mulch down is not essential this year, but it is good if you can do it. You can also mulch with non-nutrient-rich mulches, like bark-chips, which still suppress weeds and keep everything moist. Make sure everything is watered well before you mulch. In subsequent years, the need to mulch will be greater, and so it's worth sourcing a good supplier now (remember that a weed-suppressing mulch is useless if it is full of weed seeds, so do your homework and if in doubt, don't use it).

DIVIDING PERENNIALS Again, perhaps not essential for this first year (unless you are lucky enough to have inherited herbaceous perennials) but in the second year onwards you can lift your perennials out of the soil and divide them into more plants at no extra cost. After a while certain perennials get too big and congested and begin to lose their vigour. The best thing you can do for a plant like this is to divide it into little pieces.

First, identify the plant so that you know what you're dealing with. This method works for most fibrous-rooted perennials (like geraniums). Simply dig up the entire clump, lay it on a tray or path and prise the roots apart, either with your hands or lever them apart using two forks, placed back to back. You can continue dividing the clump until each bit constitutes one plantlet and a few roots, but bear in mind that the larger each clump is, the quicker it will re-establish itself. Now you can re-plant your divided plant into different places in the garden, remembering to keep each piece at roughly the same level as it was originally, and to water it in well.

PUTTING UP SUPPORTS The climbers on which you have set your heart are going to need something to scramble up, so put up either some trellis or wire. A power drill with a masonry bit, wall-plugs, vine-eye screws and, of course, wires are all you need to create a simple framework. Horizontal wires at 30cm intervals work for most climbers.

REINING YOURSELF IN Lastly, if you've given over part of your space to growing food, then this month is a busy one for planning, getting the soil right, planting and sowing. My advice, if you're new to vegetable growing, is not to try to do too much. A gorgeous vegetable patch that's productive all year round is more labour-intensive than you'd ever think possible. It needs daily work, love and attention, so if you're time-poor, then please start small, with easy veg (see shallots on page 38, spinach on page 158 and new potatoes on page 258), because if you have dreams of Villandry and a staff of only one, I'm sorry, but you're bound to be disappointed.

Sweet peas for summer

It was a packet of sweet pea seeds that gave me the gardening bug. I had never grown anything before and this, my first foray into sowing and growing plants, was a resounding success, giving me little bundles of sweetly scented blooms day after day and more importantly, the confidence and hunger to do more gardening. The Latin name for a sweet pea is *Lathyrus odoratus* and what I didn't know then is that because it's a hardy annual, it germinates easily, and grows quickly in order to make the most of its short but glorious life.

I sow my sweet peas in March (my favourite variety is still the blushing purple, strongly-scented 'Matucana'), and I would suggest that sowing your own sweet peas is a must if you are a seed-raising virgin because they are so wonderfully obliging – just follow the instructions on the packet – but I also buy ready-grown seedlings at this time too, which I can put straight in the ground or in a container without the faff and worry of raising them from babyhood. If you're very busy, this is a godsend and not expensive. There are strong, healthy seedlings appearing at most good garden centres right now, so go and snap up your favourites before someone else does.

I was planning a hedge in my new garden and decided to use a sweet pea screen both to give me an idea of how a hedge would feel, and to fill the empty space during the spring and summer (the best time for planting hedges is in the autumn and winter). This method is for a screen but you can use these climbing wonders to clothe any type of twiggy or net-like support that you choose.

YOU WILL NEED **Sweet pea seedlings** In plugs or pots from the garden centre, or grown from seed by you.
Really well-prepared soil These are hungry plants so prepare the ground really well before you start by digging a trench, at least a spade's depth, and adding some soil-improver or really well-rotted manure (see page 17).
A climbing frame I use pea sticks (made of willow or hazel and available at good nurseries) stuck into the ground at regular intervals. This is the easiest option, but some sturdy posts driven into the ground with netting stapled to them, or an old bit of fencing or trellis, works just as well. Height-wise, I would expect them to climb 1.5–2 metres.
Some garden twine
Liquid tomato food

METHOD Make sure your seedlings are really well watered in their pots. I put them in a tray of water to soak while I prepare their bed. Make a trench in your newly dug soil and very carefully remove the seedlings from their pots. If there is more than one seedling in the pot don't try to separate them. (A sweet pea will really resent you if you mess with its roots.)

Place the plants at regular intervals – 20cm apart is fine – making sure they end up at the same depth they were in their pots. Now firm the soil in gently around them and give them a really good soaking in their new home. Over the next few days, depending on the size of the plants, you'll need to tie the shoots gently into your support so they know to climb upwards, otherwise they'll just sprawl along the ground.

Once they've taken hold, if you keep watering them, they'll go rampant and cover your support in no time. When they start flowering, give them some tomato food to promote even more flowers about once a week; just follow the instructions on the bottle, adding the food to your watering can.

MORE You could sow more seeds in April or May directly into the ground between the established plants to give you more flowers later in the season. You can also grow sweet peas in a container – just make sure it is at least 30cm deep and use a half-and-half mixture of peat-free multi-purpose compost and John Innes No. 2.

Whatever you do, remember to pick the flowers, because the more you pick, the more the plant will produce. The important thing is not to let the flowers set seed (when the petals fall off and the flower turns into what looks like a silky mangetout). Producing these seeds takes up loads of energy from the plant, and it will stop bothering to make more flowers. If you keep cutting the flowers before they set seed, the plant will keep trying to make seed and therefore produce more flowers.

Shallots, for the best risotto ever

Shallots are basically an onion's slimmer, chicer, more sophisticated cousin. This is not in any way to do an onion down; it's just to say that there are times (like risotto-making times) when only a shallot will do. The taste is sweeter but with an almost vinegary sharpness to it – I'm not a supertaster by any means, but I can tell the difference.

Shallots are very easy to grow and expensive to buy in the shops, and they also store really well – all good things. They are members of the onion family and are grown either from seed (only necessary if you want to farm shallots) or special bulbs called sets, which are by far the easier option. Your sets will be one of two species: *Allium cepa* Aggregatum Group; or *Allium oschaninii*. Some people feel that the *Allium oschaninii* is the only 'true' shallot but I tend to find anything I've grown myself is the 'best' thing I've ever tasted, so I just plant whatever I find in the shops.

You won't need much space to grow a good crop – I planted 10 sets this year and got about 70 shallots (quite enough, thank you). They do well in pots too, so lack of space is neither a problem, nor an excuse.

YOU WILL NEED **Some shallot sets of whatever variety takes your fancy** These are widely available in packets from all good nurseries and online suppliers.

For growing in the ground
A nice bit of well-drained, fertile soil If you have a little vegetable patch, then you may have dug it over with a bit of manure before you started – that's good. Basically, you can put them pretty much anywhere. The only thing they don't like is compacted, claggy, clayey soil, or very acidic soil.

For growing in a container
John Innes No. 2 compost, with some added grit
A wide pot or window-box You need to plant your sets 15–18cm apart, so 5 to 6 sets in a metre-long window-box, or 2 to 3 sets in a pot with a 30cm diameter.

METHOD Make a small trench or hole in the compost or soil, depending on whether you are planting in rows or otherwise, and carefully place each set in the depression, pointy side up, and being careful not to damage its roots. Plant them so their tops are just underneath the surface. Firm down gently, water and wait. This one set will multiply and become eight or ten little shallots for you to eat. If you plant in early spring, you'll be pulling gorgeous little bulbs by the beginning of July. They will have pushed themselves up almost out of the soil, as if to say, 'Take me, I'm yours!'

Of course, you'll want to use your shallots right there and then (to make the sexiest vinaigrette, dice them super-fine and add to oil and good vinegar), but it's also a great idea to store them. To do this, just shake off the excess dirt (but don't bother to separate the bulbs) and lay them somewhere dry in the sun for a week or so, or inside your kitchen window-sill if it's raining. Then store them in a cool, dry place, checking them regularly to make sure there are no 'rotters'. I lay mine out in a wooden box, making sure they're not touching.

MORE   As the weather turns cold, it's risotto time, and nothing brings back the summer months like a lemon risotto. Sweat three or four finely chopped shallots in butter, add a cup of risotto rice, coating the grains with the fat, and a glass of decent white wine. Start stirring gently and add hot chicken or vegetable stock, ladleful by ladleful, letting the rice absorb the liquid until the rice is how you like it. Then put in the juice and rind of one lemon, along with an obscene amount of butter. Sprinkle generously with parsley and eat with your feet curled up underneath you.

Petunia bombs

You know those glorious hanging baskets of petunias outside pubs? I've always loved them, and if the pub landlord can do it, then so can you and I. Petunias are ideal hanging basket candidates because they bloom like erupting volcanoes, spilling over the sides, and if you choose a large trailing cultivar, it will cover the basket completely and you end up with what looks like a spherical flower bomb. I love to hang them in trees and use them like outdoor chandeliers. Equally, if you have a strong arm, you can take them down and rest them on an empty pot in the middle of a table for an instant gawp-at-me centrepiece.

Petunias are part of the potato family. Most are perennial, but we grow them as annuals because they get nuked by our winters. They have been expanded by man into many different cultivars, all of which have these floppy, velvety trumpet flowers, incredible colours and a certain sticky hairiness which should not, by the way, put you off growing them. The whole point of a petunia is that it is over-the-top and 'blowsy', so don't even think of trying to be boringly tasteful because you won't manage it.

YOU WILL NEED **Petunia plants** These are sold as bedding in polystyrene six-packs from March onwards. For a hanging basket of 45cm diameter, I use 10 plants, but get some extra to keep in reserve just in case you lose any to drought or slugs.

A large hanging basket The larger the better I find, because the fewer the baskets, the easier the watering, and because larger is more spectacular in this case.

An empty flowerpot To rest your hanging basket on as you plant it up.

Multi-purpose compost You can either buy special compost specifically formulated for hanging baskets, or mix ordinary peat-free multi-purpose compost with some water-retaining gel granules and some fertiliser granules (available in any good garden centre).

A sturdy bracket This must be attached really well to a wall by someone who knows what they are doing, or a butcher's S hook that will fit over a strong tree branch – hanging baskets are really, really heavy when they're watered.

Liquid tomato food or seaweed extract (Optional.)

METHOD First, put your hanging basket on the empty flowerpot to stop it rolling around while you plant it up. If you've got ready-mixed hanging basket compost, complete with water-retaining gel inside, then go right ahead and fill your basket. If not, then mix the compost with the water-retaining granules and fertiliser granules according to the instructions. Now fill your hanging basket with the mixed compost so it comes up 5cm or so shy of the rim, water it really well and leave it for an hour. This will give the granules a chance to expand before you put your plants in. If you plant them before you've watered, the granules are likely to push the plants up and out of the basket. While you're waiting, put the polystyrene cells in a tray of water to get the petunia plants properly saturated.

When you're ready to plant, carefully push each seedling out of its cell with your fingers, and make a hole big enough for it in the compost, also with your fingers, pushing the plant in and firming it down. Space them evenly, but closer together than indicated on the label; to get a great profusion of flowers, you need to over-plant slightly. Fill in any gaps with more compost and firm everything in really well. To make watering easy, there should be 2cm between the top of the compost and the rim of the basket.

Now hang your basket up and just keep watering it. When it's really warm and sunny, you're going to have to do this twice a day – hanging baskets are ridiculously high-maintenance, even with gel inside them. A liquid feed can't hurt either – remember that these plants are not required to toughen up for winter, or even to stand upright, they just need to shine for one season, so they can be as soft and sappy as they like, as long as they produce masses of flowers and foliage. I feed my baskets about once a fortnight (I'd feed them more if I remembered).

MORE Other plants you could add into the mix are begonias and zonal pelargoniums, and any trailing foliage looks great. Keep it big and gaudy though.

An easy compost bay

This one bit of easy DIY will produce the engine of your garden – compost is that important. If you can't bear the thought of having one of the council's free plastic monstrosities in your garden, then this is a perfect alternative; it's easy to knock up, almost totally free, far more capacious, and much prettier than plastic (I think). My aim here is to give you the means to a compost bay as quickly as possible, which is why there are no saws or spirit levels involved … if you're ace at DIY then you'll probably want to skip this page and build something far more accomplished.

YOU WILL NEED   **Four wooden builders' pallets.** These are ubiquitous in urban areas, often stacked up in the road outside homes which are being renovated. Ask the builder nicely and he'll probably give you some. Or you can find them in big builders' merchants.
Heavy-duty plastic-coated wire
Wire cutters
A pair of pliers
A roll of chicken wire 1m wide
A hammer
Metal tacks

METHOD   First decide where to put your compost bay. Ideally, it will be against a wall, where it is easily accessible but out of sight. You can put your compost bay on top of stone or concrete, but it's better if it's on bare ground, so that the worms can find it. To make the bay, you just attach each pallet to its neighbour at right angles, so that you end up with a bottomless square bay into which you will toss your garden waste. Use wire at the top and bottom of each pallet to attach them together, and pliers to twist and tighten the join. When you've attached the first three pallets, line the inside with chicken wire, hammering in tacks to keep it in place along the top and bottom. Now cut another square of chicken wire and attach it to the last pallet separately. This will be the 'door' to your compost bay so it must be removable. Finally, attach the last side to the bay, again using wire, but this time making sure the ends are within easy reach so you can undo them whenever you want.

TO MAKE COMPOST   It's worth saying right from the outset that the more time you lavish on your compost heap, the quicker you'll get usable compost, and the better it will be. A very quick exploration into how compost is created will tell you that your garden and food waste gets eaten by masses of micro-organisms (fungi and bacteria) which are eaten in turn by slightly bigger things, like protozoa, nematodes and mites. These are then eaten by other, bigger things, like beetles and millipedes, so you have to imagine that you're a party organiser, charged with providing a great environment for a massive eating orgy. The main elements for the perfect party are: air (why you turn your compost heap); water (why you keep it moist); food (why you chuck in a wide variety of material); small portions (why you chop things up).

Start your compost heap by putting a few twiggy bits right at the bottom, which allows airflow underneath, and then just start tossing in all your plant waste. The exceptions to this are: perennial weeds and annual weeds that have flowered (these, I soak in water for three weeks until they are well and truly dead, and then I add the water to my pots and the slimy remains to the compost); anything diseased (like rose leaves with black-spot, which should be burned or thrown out with the rubbish); and any food from the kitchen, other than raw fruit and vegetables. Also, don't put thick branches or thorny things in unless you've shredded them because they'll take an age to break down. You can also put cardboard and paper in the heap as long as it's torn up into bits and not shiny in any way.

If you have time, cut everything up as small as possible, and keep ringing the changes – a thin layer of one thing should be followed by something different to create balance. Try to get a good mix of wet and dry material so that all the tiny micro-organisms can get to work and the whole thing will heat up, which will help to break it all down. Balance is everything – it should be neither too wet, nor too dry, neither too twiggy, nor too slimy, and it will only attract vermin or become unpleasantly smelly if you put in cooked food, meat or fish. It's not an exact science, so your first compost heap (like your first anything) will involve normal, healthy amounts of trial and error.

In terms of when your compost is ready, let instinct be your guide – you'll know when it looks, feels and smells just right. The more you mix your compost heap, the quicker it will break down, but in reality, most of us have neither the time nor the inclination for this, and it's fine to wait until it's full before you open the door, get the whole lot out and have a jolly good, calorie-burning go at it before putting it all back in, and waiting for the magic to happen. If you make your compost carefully, and mix it well, you'll have usable black stuff to spread on your flowerbeds this time next year. Some of your larger clippings may need more time, so just return these to the heap. Some people take usable compost from the bottom of the heap, whilst continuing to add to the top of it. Others have two bays, using one and filling the other.

Turn over for pictures

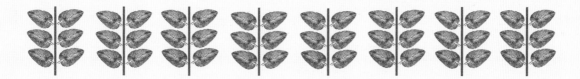

Pea shoots for sexy salad

This is the most delicious green of the summer for me, and the best thing about them is that you can continue sowing and growing these long into autumn for a sweet, crunchy snack. They also look utterly fabulous whilst growing in their container on your terrace or outside window-sill, or cut and put in a vase with other flowers.

YOU WILL NEED **A packet of pea seeds** These are just dried peas, and you can get a big box much more cheaply from the supermarket. If you're planning on doing vast swathes of pea shoots, then that's probably a good idea. I like trying different varieties in small pots and choosing my favourite flavour, so I buy them in seed packets from the garden centre.
A shallow, wide pot or a window-box The more surface area the better, and because you're not going to need the peas to grow up to their full height, you don't need to worry about giving them much root space.
Some multi-purpose compost

METHOD Fill your pot with the compost so it comes about 5cm shy of the top of the container. Spread the peas all over the surface of the compost, making sure they're packed closely together but in one layer, and cover them with another layer of compost (about 2cm should do it). Pat it down approvingly, water and wait.

Keep watering daily and, within days, you should see shoots peeping through. Some multi-purpose composts are made up of quite big 'bits' and if yours is like this, then it's likely the shoots will raise the surface all in one piece, like the crust of a cake. If this happens, then very gently break the compost up, prodding it slightly to get it down in between the shoots as they grow.

Your shoots should be ready for harvesting whenever you see fit (keep tasting along the way). I prefer to wait until the beautiful climbing tendrils have formed, and then I either chop from just above the surface of the compost, or literally pull the whole lot up, wash it and serve it with its seed attached.

Turn over for more pictures

Raised beds for your flowers and veg

Okay, here's a bit of DIY that's worth doing, and which will save you real money. If you're planning on growing vegetables in your garden, a raised bed system will help you keep things under control in a way that makes this more than worth the effort.

A raised bed is simply a 'box' with no bottom, placed on the open ground and filled with weed-free compost so that your plants (and particularly your root vegetables) can benefit from extra-luxe, extra-deep, extra-moist soil. It's basically a five-star hotel for plants. Because it has 'sides', watering is easier because it doesn't drain away to the edge of the beds, and weeds are less of an issue because you'll have filled it with sterile compost. It also makes you feel better, because it looks neat and tidy and under control. You can of course buy ready-made raised bed systems from a variety of places and they're great, but making your own is quite easy and a lot cheaper. Before you begin, here are three helpful suggestions to make things easier in the long term:

1   Remember to leave enough room between raised beds for a wheelbarrow and – if your paths are grass – a lawn-mower.
2   It's a good idea to keep the beds a maximum of 150cm wide, otherwise you'll have trouble reaching the middle.
3   If you're using timber that comes in set measurements, like scaffold planks, then size the beds accordingly so you don't have to do so much sawing.

YOU WILL NEED   **Some timber** The possibilities are manifold but there are some general rules (see opposite). The amount will depend on the size of your raised beds.
A saw To cut your planks to size.
A hammer To remove any nails or other annoying things stuck in your timber. Scaffolding planks have horrible metal 'ends' that you'll need to remove carefully before you start.
Some really long screws
A power drill with a screw-driver bit
A long extension lead (Optional.)
A half-moon lawn edger or bamboo canes and string
A good, sharp spade For digging trenches.
A spirit level

Super-luxe, top-quality organic loam-based compost This is weed-free and sterile. You can either buy this in bags from the garden centre (labelled 'topsoil') or order it from a reputable supplier.

Well-rotted horse-manure To enrich the soil.

A helper or two

METHOD A word about wood: first, it should be untreated. Lots of wood is treated with chemicals to give it longevity. This is fine in other parts of the garden, but not, I think, near plants that are going to end up, often in their delicious raw state, on your plate. This means that, yes, your timber will have a 'life span' and will eventually rot into the ground, but not for years and years, by which time you will probably want something entirely different anyway. Locally sourced, used wood is always more sustainable than new. The 'planks' should be at least 2cm thick and 30cm wide. They can of course be much thicker and wider if you want. Lastly, the wood should be a hard wood (i.e. durable, and not brittle). I use old scaffold planks.

First, cut your planks to size, taking care not to harm yourself in the process. Place the end of one plank at right angles to the next. Get someone to help you hold them together and drive a screw through the side of one plank and into the end of the next, until you have what looks like a shallow, bottomless 'box'.

Now lay the whole thing on the patch of ground where you want it to go, taking care with it, because it won't be at all stable until it's in its trench. You need to 'draw' around it, so that you can slot it into the ground. I use a lawn edger, which cuts right up against the vertical edge, but some bamboo canes with string would work too. Using this line as your guide, dig a trench for your wooden frame, plunging the spade in as vertically as possible. It doesn't have to be very deep – just enough to bury your chosen plank by one-third so that it is supported by the (more compacted) soil on the outside that will eventually form your path.

You can now slot the frame into the ground, making sure it's exactly level by using a spirit level. You'll need to do some adjusting here, some adding and subtracting of earth, because, unless you are a robot, you will inevitably have dug too deeply in some places and too shallowly in others. The ultimate goal is to get it sitting in its trench and stable, so you can walk along its edge like a tight-rope artist without it wobbling.

Once you're satisfied you can single-dig the inside with the manure, so it's lovely and crumbly and all traces of weeds are gone gone gone. (See page 17 for instructions on how to single-dig.) Now tamp the soil down by shuffling over it Charlie Chaplin style, so that it's firm, but not compacted. The earth inside the bed should be higher than that outside, because you've dug in the manure, and now all you need to do is fill it up to the top with the new compost. These brand-new beds will look so beautiful, but I warn you to get planting as soon as possible, because nature, abhorring a vacuum, will send weeds to party in your empty beds.

Lovage, parsley with punch

Once you've planted a bit of lovage and started using it in the kitchen, you'll wonder how you ever did without it. *Levisticum officinale* is a hardy perennial, which means that once you've planted some, it'll come back year after year. It can get really quite big, but you don't have to let it – just keep it well clipped. You can grow lovage from seed really easily, but since this plant is a perennial, and can be increased by division, buying a ready-grown plant is a sound investment. The flavour is a knock-out combination of celery, parsley, aniseed and lemon, and it often comes to my rescue when I don't have the time or inclination to gather the necessary for a bouquet garni. An onion, a carrot, some peppercorns and a bunch of lovage are often the sum of what gets thrown in a stockpot or soup, and the results are always tasty. My absolute favourite lovage recipe, which I include opposite, has lovage as the main ingredient – enjoy.

YOU WILL NEED **A lovage plant** They're widely available and really easy to grow, so you will need only one.

For growing in the ground
A nice bit of soil Lovage likes the classic combination of moist but well-drained, rich soil. So, if your garden soil is dry or sandy, then you'll need to add some well-rotted manure or soil-improver to beef it up.
A sunny or partially shady site Close to the kitchen is useful, because this is your emergency go-to herb for when it's pelting with rain or you just can't be bothered.

For container growing
A container that is at least 30cm diameter You may want to start your lovage in here and then re-plant it when it outgrows its pot. Eventually, it will be happier in a larger pot, but it will take a couple of years for it to reach maturity.
Compost John Innes No. 2 mixed half-and-half with multi-purpose compost.

METHOD Plant your lovage in its pot or allotted space and water it in really well. Give it a couple of weeks to get used to its new home and then start harvesting from it, gingerly at first. The flavour will change after mid-summer when the plant flowers. Some find this post-flowering flavour bitter but personally I love it. For the sauce opposite, though, do use the younger leaves, harvested before flowering. The plant will die down over winter, then re-sprout and delight you next spring.

MORE Mark Diacono is the man behind the vegetable garden at River Cottage. He also owns Otter Farm, where he grows and sells all manner of extraordinary plants. This lovage sauce is taken from his brilliant *River Cottage Handbook No.4: Veg Patch*. It goes with pretty much anything but is particularly fine with fish.

Add a dozen finely chopped lovage leaves to a couple of generous knobs of bubbling butter in a pan and cook for 3 minutes. Add half a glass of good white wine and simmer for another couple of minutes. Finally, stir in a teaspoon of grainy mustard and season well.

Clematis wigwams

I used to shy away from clematis because I was put off by reading about all their pruning requirements. Dire warnings about clematis wilt and how you must or mustn't plant it too deep had led me to file it away in my brain as 'difficult'. And then I saw someone on telly who grew hundreds of different clematis varieties, all of them in pots. This was all the encouragement I needed. It is not only possible, but extremely easy to grow clematis in pots for beautiful, flower-festooned columns, or to plonk them in your flowerbeds for added glamour. You just need to pick the right variety.

Clematis is such a vast genus that it is split into groups. There are the early-flowering species, which tend to be very vigorous, and need more space than a pot can give. Then there are the early-to-mid-season species and, lastly, the late, large-flowered cultivars. Groups two and three are the ones to choose from if you want a clematis column, or want to grow clematis in a container. And if you want to plonk one in the ground, then follow my planting instructions, give it a climbing frame and watch it go.

YOU WILL NEED
A clematis plant Group two or three; it will tell you on the label.
Really good, free-draining compost I use John Innes No. 3.
Horticultural grit I add three generous handfuls to my pot.
A large, deep pot Mine are 30cm wide and 40cm deep, but if you want bigger wigwams at the bottom then choose a wider pot.
Some crocks As you're using soil-based compost, which is very heavy, I would add some pieces of broken pot or a few bits of polystyrene to stop the holes in the bottom of your container blocking up.
Three or more bamboo canes Around 2 metres long, or you can buy ready-made obelisks to put in pots from most garden centres.
String
Gravel mulch Pea-sized or larger – available to buy in bags (optional).

METHOD
Mix up the compost with the grit. Add crocks to the bottom of your pot and fill it half-full with compost. Now put your clematis plant on top to check the height. You need to plant the clematis 3–5cm deeper than it is in its plastic pot, making sure you leave 3cm between the rim of the pot and the surface of the compost so that you can water it efficiently. Remove the plant carefully from its plastic, and plant it, filling in around the sides and firming it in gently. Now place the canes around the edge of the pot at equal intervals, and tie them together at the top with string to form a wigwam.

If you've got a plant that looks in any way leggy and damaged, you can cut back the stems to just above a bud about 30cm above the surface of the soil. Take the stems of the plant and very gently coax each one in the direction of a bamboo cane, tying them very gently and loosely. The aim is to have each stem spiralling up a bamboo cane. This will mean keeping an eye on it to make sure those twining leaf stalks are going where you want them to, and tying them in gently if necessary. Your wigwam should be covered in leaves by midsummer. The timing of the flowers depends on the type of clematis you have chosen. You can feed your plant with liquid fertiliser both before and after it has flowered, but don't feed it while it's flowering, or it'll just put on lots of leaves and no flowers. The bottom will be less well-covered than the top, but that doesn't matter because this plant is all about height and those dinner-plate flowers.

Remember to water regularly, and if possible, site the pot so that the bottom is in the shade and only the wigwam is in the sun. This will help to keep the roots cool, which is what they like best. I simulate this on my terrace by surrounding the pot with other pots to keep the sun from hitting the sides, and adding a layer of gravel mulch over the top of the compost.

Pruning is much easier than it seems. Here's how I simplified it for myself: is your clematis one of the large, evergreen ones that flowers early in spring? If so, then leave it alone. Is it starting to flower in late spring and early summer? If so, then perform some surgery in late winter or very early spring, removing all the dead stuff and cutting any living shoots back to just above a good strong bud – the bud you like the best. Does it flower in the summer and early autumn? If so, then this is the easiest one to prune – just hack the whole thing back to just above the bud that's closest to 20cm above the ground also in late winter or early spring.

Shrub roses for scented bouquets

One of the most exciting things about having more space in my new garden was the thought of growing roses in the kind of quantities that would give me posies throughout the summer, not just for myself, but enough for me to give away to my favourite people too. Although shrub roses can easily be grown in a pot, I had so little room on my balcony that anything I had there needed to be 'brush-past-able', which meant that thorniness was a no-no. I satisfied my rosy craving well enough with a climbing 'Madame Isaac Pereire' around my front door (and a bit of furious hinting to the Hunk whenever we passed a florist). For the new garden, my first outing was to a specialist rose nursery, as my plan was that they would form, if not the backbone, then at least a large part of the muscle in the garden. They were the very first plants to go in, and I have not been disappointed. They went in the ground at the end of February and the beginning of March, and by June I was completely over-run with roses. Here is my method for growing a shrub rose, along with some of my favourite scented varieties for picking.

Roses are long-lived, tough plants, so it's worth doing a bit of research into what you want and satisfy your heart's desire by ordering it, rather than just buying one you like the look of on impulse. That said, don't spend too long looking – there are so many beautiful roses out there you might be 'researching' for years. This is the perfect time to plant roses, but not the perfect time to see or smell them, because they're not out yet, so unless you want to wait a year and pick your favourites whilst they're in bloom (which I most certainly did not), then I advise you to do the following:

1   Find a book of roses or a catalogue, or trawl the internet and gorge yourself on the look of them (see page 280 for websites). Mark down ones you like and soon you'll detect which shapes and forms most float your boat. You will notice that the books have lots of descriptions for different forms (damask, centifolia, noisette, bourbon, etc.), but I can broadly categorise rose shapes into four groups: shallow cup shapes; bowl-like, cabbagey, almost spherical shapes; wide-open show-me-your-stamen shapes; and 'All because the lady loves Cadbury's Milk Tray' shapes (or classic hybrid tea roses).

2   Decide which colours you don't want, rather than which colours you do. This leaves your options nice and open.

3   Think about scent and don't get too poncey about it. For me, a rose has got to be scented to earn a place in my space, and for it to be anything other than 'strongly scented', that scent has to blow me away – end of story. Some people, though, fall in love with the look of a rose so much that they don't mind it being unscented. This hasn't happened to me yet.

4   Think about disease resistance. For me, this is boring but important – so important, in fact, that I rejected a lot of my first choices because a bit of research showed them up to be prone to mildew, black-spot, and other nasties. Don't be seduced by rarity and delicacy; this usually denotes roses that are super-difficult to grow. These will not give you any pleasure, not ever, so leave them to the experts.

So, armed with your shape, colour and scent preferences, and after a bit of soul-searching about how much husbandry you are prepared to commit to in terms of keeping your rose healthy (in my case, very little), then you should seek out a really good rose nursery or get on the telephone to talk to someone who can advise you. If there's a particular rose you're intent on buying, no matter what, then ask them about it anyway – plant people love to share knowledge about plants. I was lucky to go to a nursery run by a lady who actually *told* me what to get, once we'd established that it had to be cabbage-shaped, deeply scented and tough. I was thrilled because too much choice rather sends me into a spin and I love having someone a bit bossy around to set me straight. I came away with roses I had never heard of and some that I would never have bought in a million years had she not ordered me to, including a stunning blush-coloured beauty that is stinking the room out beautifully as I write.

The rules for growing roses are really simple:

1   Plant them during the winter and early spring (right now is perfect).

2   Prepare the planting hole with indulgent care. Dig a large hole twice the size of the pot, mixing a couple of generous handfuls of good, well-rotted manure in with the soil at the bottom of the hole. Make sure it's really well mixed, otherwise the manure will scorch the roots.

3   Firm it in well, using your foot around the stem to make sure it's secure.

4   Water it in well, and keep watering daily for around a week, and then every other day for another week or so, until you can see that the plant has started growing.

5   As the weather warms up, go out and check the forming buds for aphids, squishing any that you see, or spraying them with a jet of water.

6 Feed them during the growing season with a liquid fertiliser, or you can get one specially formulated for roses, following the instructions. I must add to this that I didn't feed mine at all in their first year and I got masses of roses, so it's not essential.

7 Deadhead the spent blooms as soon as they go over by either nipping them off just under the bloom, or cutting them back to the first pair of leaves. This will ensure they carry on blooming for as long as possible.

8 Pruning roses doesn't have to be scary or complicated. There is masses of conflicting advice about it. The simple fact is that the most gorgeous of all roses are the ones that are left un-pruned to flower abundantly. Of course, we need to constrain them a bit so they fit into the space we are willing to give them.

I was taught to prune roses hard and close to the ground, but then I read a book by Bob Flowerdew called *The No-Work Garden* (you can see why that appealed to me) in which he explained brilliantly why this method creates a rod for the gardener's own back. Hard-pruning and feeding the plant creates lots of sap that attracts aphids, which in turn makes it a cinch for fungi to get into the plant, so then you have to spray it. The strong re-growth prompted by hard-pruning causes 'wind rock', which weakens the plant and eventually kills it – a vicious cycle of hard work and buying replacement roses.

Some of my roses, planted in February and March, were still flowering well into November. I pruned them lightly in November (and a few as late as January) at about waist-height, just above a bud. I put a bit of well-rotted manure around the bottom of each one in March, and instead of getting just a few big blooms, I got masses of smaller ones, produced in separate flushes on shorter shoots, but then I'm not producing roses to be sold in shops or to win prizes … I just want them in a bowl by my bed, thank you very much. The message here is, as always, to be gentle and to go with your instinct.

April

The blossom this year has been utterly magnificent and totally over the top, which is the result partly of the very cold winter we've just had, and partly of my having inherited four blossoming trees, making me notice it all the more. By the second week in April, I've done most of the planting, in quite a rush, reminding myself constantly that plants are not like bricks and mortar – if it's in the wrong place, I can simply move it.

The plants that came with me from my old balcony have gone in, along with loads of perennials in small pots. An embarrassment of delphiniums have gone in, in groups of three or five, and lots of *Stachys* (lamb's ears), planted in the spaces underneath the tall tripods that punctuate the flowerbeds, loads of wafty *Hesperis* (sweet rocket) and masses of *Nepeta* (catmint) – this is rather foolhardy because the neighbourhood cats are a problem, but I can't help loving the *Nepeta*, so something's got to give. I've also put in six naughtily bought, and therefore highly prized, bearded irises, each a different colour. *Lychnis coronaria* has been planted in bulk, along with poppies galore and lots of *Alchemilla mollis* (lady's mantle). There are *Phlox, Rudbeckia, Eryngium* and *Lavatera*, a large order of hardy geraniums, and in The Apple Garden I have planted ferns, *Primula* and as many *Pulmonaria* as I can afford. The list goes on, and it's possibly apparent that pared down is not my style.

By the end of the month, I'm tinkering about with the planting again, just to accommodate the odd impulse-buy (we are, after all, human, and where's the fun of working to a plan if there's no room for deviation?) One of these purchases is an allium – just one, because they are hugely expensive to buy in pots (much better to plant them as bulbs in the autumn), but I can't quite get through the year without having just *one*. Things are beginning to look 'bedded in', but there are still gaps to fill. I haven't got round to sowing hardy annuals yet, but May is not too late, and in fact, it's better to be a bit tardy than to sow too early. I'm not going to sweat it, though, because there is always plenty of bedding on sale throughout the early summer specifically designed to fill gaps.

One thing I have managed to do is to sow hardy annuals in one of the raised beds that the Hunk and I made together. These were originally designed to hold vegetables on a crop-rotation system, but I thought better of it, valuing as I do, my time and sanity. I'm fond of the odd luxurious morsel as long as it looks pretty, but I'd far rather have a garden full of flowers than potatoes, so I've given over two of the raised beds to flowers, and one is to become a herb garden. The other will have onions and shallots, salads and new potatoes; and any other vegetables will go in pots or gaps in the borders.

WHAT TO DO IN YOUR VIRGIN GARDEN THIS MONTH

WEEDING   Boring old weeds. Now that everything is warming up and the sun has begun to shine, little seedlings (or weedlings, as I like to call them) will be coming up in their thousands. They need to be kept under control – not so you spend every second pulling every last weed out, but just so they don't get big enough to starve your other plants of any light or nutrients. My favourite tool for weed destruction is a little hand hoe (see page 24).

With a hoe, you can slide it just a centimetre or so into the soil in one clean sweeping action, and in doing so, the blade cuts or uproots all the tiny weedlings in its path, leaving them lying on the surface of the soil for the sun to frazzle at its leisure. It's important, therefore, to choose a sunny day (or at least a dry one) to do your hoeing, and I would also heartily recommend an old cushion to kneel on, and some good tunes on the iPod. I'm always flabbergasted how quickly it gets done and a bit embarrassed at how much I enjoy it. As with many things, thinking about doing the hoeing is much more unpleasant than actually doing it.

The most effective way to control weeds, however, is to avoid bare earth. The sooner you plant something, the sooner you can say goodbye to your hoe. (See below for my favourite gap-fillers.)

BULBS   Unless you started your garden in the autumn, or your budget stretches to buying ready-grown bulbs, then the one thing you'll miss out on this year is the wondrous spring show they give. Don't worry, because you're going to plant lots of bulbs for next year (see page 120), and you can also fill gaps with bedding (see opposite), so you won't miss them this time round. If you absolutely cannot live without the sight of a tulip or an allium, then go ahead and buy one or two, like I did, as a special treat to remind you of what's in store next year. You can still get bulbous though, because this is a great time to buy and get in the ground summer-flowering bulbs to flesh out your planting. My absolute favourite is *Gladiolus callianthus* (sometimes called *Acidanthera* – see page 122), but lilies, *Canna*, *Agapanthus* and those marvellous frilly gladioli can all be planted now. Make sure the soil is warm before you plant – warm enough to sit on with your bare bottom is a good indication – but if you need a number, then get a soil thermometer and make sure it reads 13°C or above.

It's easy to fill a garden with spring and summer perennials, thinking that autumn will never come, and who could blame you if you left out the suggested late-summer and autumn wonders from your shopping list, but if you can bear to look up and source some of these plants, you will have done yourself an enormous favour. (When the sun is shining and you've got that holiday feeling, it's easy for the garden to look good, but when the weather turns and things get serious again, having some late-summer stalwarts will feel totally essential.) Here are my easy, obliging, make-a-splash favourites: *Anemone x hybrida* (Japanese anemone – see page 208 for more on this); *Aster x frikartii* 'Mönch'; *Dahlia*; *Echinacea*; *Erigeron* (fleabane); *Gaura*; *Geranium*; *Helenium*; and *Rudbeckia*.

But, if you don't mind a bit of a calming down in autumn – and as long as you've planted a good variety of evergreen and deciduous shrubs, and dotted them through with lots of star perennials – then all you need to organise is how you want to fill in your gaps.

You can do this either by buying summer bedding from the garden centre (plants grown specifically to look good over the summer months and then to be thrown on the compost heap), or by sowing hardy annuals, or a mixture of both. For a new garden, summer bedding is a godsend because it's a quick, beautiful and cheap way to fill in those gaps instantly while your new plants (particularly your shrubs) are growing, and keeps the weeds under control at the same time. One day, that small philadelphus is going to be a large bush covered in sweetly scented white flowers. Until that day, there is bedding to make your borders sing.

Here are my favourite bedding plants, all widely available: *Antirrhinum* (snapdragon); *Calendula* (marigold); *Cosmos*; *Dianthus* (pinks); *Matthiola* (stock); *Nicotiana* (tobacco plant); *Zinnia*. Always make sure that bedding is really well watered before you plant it out, and that you water it in properly, and then keep watering daily for the next few days.

If you've got grass in your patch, and you've been putting it off, then you've really got to mow your lawn. I promise you, there are few things in life that make you feel better than having mowed a lawn (for me, it feels almost as good as tidying my knicker drawer), and the smell is absolute magic too. For pleasurable mowing, preparation is key: go round and remove any sticks and stones before you start, and do try to find a good lawnmower, either to rent, borrow or buy, because heavy, blunt, awkward machines are life-sapping. Good-quality mowers are not expensive, particularly if you club together with a neighbour or three to buy one. I'm not a lawn lady, and actively don't want an immaculate one, but there is a whole industry built around beautiful swards, so if that's your thing, there's plenty to keep you happy for the rest of your life on that score.

WATERING   Keep watering all your plants, particularly the shrubs. Their roots need to grow
down and reach the water table, and in order for them to do that, the ground
immediately surrounding them needs a good soaking on a regular basis. If you
water only a little bit, the roots stay close to the surface and the plant will never be
able to look after itself properly. It's impossible to be scientific about watering, but
in my experience, the amount of water you give to plants is far less important than
the care with which they are watered. The planting stage is the most important,
making a little dam around each shrub to guide the water to the right place (see
page 30), and for most small and medium-sized gardens, the best thing you can
do for your plants (and your water consumption) is to go round and water them
individually using a watering can. This is time-consuming initially, but pleasurable
and will pay huge dividends in the end. I make it easier for myself by filling a large
tub with water and then dipping a large can of water in to fill it. I then let the tap
run whilst I'm watering, filling the tub for the next can-ful.

I used this method for all the plants in my garden, big and small, until the
weather got really dry and I finally invested in a sprinkler. Make sure to pay
attention to hosepipe bans and the like, and also know that to give a good soaking,
you really do have to leave a sprinkler on for a couple of hours or more – anything
less is not worth the bother. The watering is indiscriminate, and therefore far less
economical, but it does save time and is great for large areas and lawns in
particular. If you've watered your plants in well at the beginning, though, they
should have enough oomph to get through dry spells. As with all things, observe
and use your instinct. It's good to know that, although plants wilt alarmingly in the
heat of the day, they mostly come back when it cools down in the evening. And
lastly, however you water, make sure you do it in the early morning or evening to
avoid evaporation and save yourself time.

Watering pots is a totally different proposition – they need daily watering in the
summer months, whatever the weather. Make things easy on yourself by always
leaving a gap between the top of the compost and the rim of the pot, and placing
a tray underneath to catch the run-off.

THINKING   If you're planning on buying a large number of the same large shrub or tree, either
ABOUT   to repeat all over the garden or to make into a hedge, then it's worth ordering
HEDGING   bare-root trees now for planting in the autumn. Bare-root trees (which have been
grown in the ground and then dug up) are much less expensive than potted ones
because they are easy to transport and need less fussing over as you plant them
in late autumn or winter. There is nothing wrong with buying plants in pots on
a whim; this is just a tip for those who are organised and decisive enough to think
miles ahead.

Hostas for leafy succulence in a pot

Hostas are perennials that hail from various different habitats, but mostly woodland, in China, Korea and Japan. They are available in garden centres from mid-spring when they're just unfurling (see picture overleaf), and in general, a hosta likes to chillax in the shade, whether it be under a tree, or in the lee of a house. This makes them perfect for smartly flanking doorways. The reason they make good pot plants is not because they enjoy being confined, but simply because a terracotta pot, particularly one surrounded by a moat, or slathered with Vaseline, or top-dressed with grit, is a bit of an obstacle course for a slug. Those fabulous, fleshy leaves are a superb addition to any pot garden, particularly mine, as I normally over-plum the pudding with the wafty, delicate and ethereal. The one thing about having a perennial in a pot, though, is that it hibernates for the winter, so I've added a few suggestions below for suitable hosta house-mates to keep things lovely whilst your plant snoozes.

YOU WILL NEED **A hosta** You can either order these online from specialist growers or go direct to a good nursery and pick your favourite. If you go now, there should be plenty of choice.
Compost I use a mixture of one-third multi-purpose and two-thirds John Innes No. 2.
A pot I use an ordinary terracotta pot of 30cm diameter, which is a good size for a hosta bought in a 3-litre pot. Obviously, you will need to re-pot as the plant expands over the years.
A box of Slug Stoppa granules These are pet and child-safe and they work by sucking out moisture from whatever they touch in a way that slugs find unbearable. If you can't find these, then avail yourself of a tub of Vaseline.

METHOD First, mix your compost and fill your pot to get it ready for its hosta. Then remove the plant from its plastic container and check it really thoroughly for slugs. Look at the base of the leaves and in all the crevices, and keep an eye out for tiny baby slugs too, because they're the ones that do the damage. It might be worth carefully rinsing the foliage with a spray of water just to make doubly sure there are no nasties lurking.

Then plant the hosta in the normal way, making sure it is planted at the same level it was in its container, and leaving 3cm or so between the top of the compost and the rim of the container. Firm it in well, and water it so you're sure it's saturated.

Place the pot where you want it to be (at least for the time being), and if you're using the granules, now is the time to pour them on. Be generous – you need a layer at least 1cm thick, and much thicker around the base of the plant. I pour mine in closely and thickly around the centre of the plant and then gently shake the leaves to get the granules to fall on to the surface of the compost. You want to create a mound around the base of your plant.

If you don't fancy the granules (and they are a pale colour, which can sometimes detract from the beauty of the leaves), then get your finger out and slather Vaseline thickly around the rim of the pot, and also about halfway down. The slugs can't normally cross a Vaselined surface, but if they want to give it a go, then good luck to them.

MORE   A hosta will die down over winter and you'll be left with what looks like an empty pot. As the leaves are dying, in late autumn, you could carefully plant some cyclamen around the edge to take you through the winter months. If you're not too busy sunbathing in late summer, you could source some autumn-flowering iris, like *Iris tuberosa*, or autumn-flowering snowflakes (*Leucojum autumnale*), the bulbs of which can both be planted in late summer for autumn flowering. Then, in the winter, you could add some snowdrops into the mix if you have room.

A cutting garden

I've always lusted after a cutting garden – somewhere I can pootle off to and return with armfuls of flowers to scent the house. The vision is somewhat romanticised and punctuated by ladies in beautiful hats, like an EM Forster novel, but the reality is that very few of us have the space to devote entirely to a pickery. By its very nature this is a place that looks slightly vandalised most of the time, but the argument for having an area just for flowers you want to pick is that you can enjoy certain blooms that may not necessarily fit with your garden's colour scheme. In addition, it's often unbearable to pick lots from the garden, and it's nice to have a profusion of flowers that are grown specifically for picking, and that you won't feel bad about removing. The ultimate flower for picking – the sweet pea – is not dealt with here, but on page 34.

The key to a cutting garden is to plant (or thin out your sowed flowers) much closer together than you might usually do. This is because you're not in it for the long-haul – in other words, you just want them for their body. Even so, you still have to treat them nicely. Here is what I planted, along with some other suggestions for how to keep your cutting patch going through the autumn and winter, and into spring.

YOU WILL NEED

Some packets of annual seed *Nigella*, cornflower and stock are all easy to grow and last well in the vase. I would also suggest you add some *Ammi majus*, which is easy to grow from seed and a pretty, cloud-like plant that looks great with everything.

Some boxes of summer bedding Make sure you choose plants that will stand up well to life in a vase (i.e. not *Lobelia* or anything lank and trailing). I'm talking about plants like snapdragons, *Cosmos* and *Dianthus* (pinks). All of these are available in polystyrene cells from good garden centres.

A suitable site, preferably in full sun I used two of my raised beds originally destined for vegetables (that didn't last long) – each is 2m x 1.5m in size. I suggest you plant half your plot with ready-grown seedlings from the garden centre, and direct-sow the seeds in the other half. This way, you can start picking pretty much immediately.

Really good, crumbly topsoil This must be lump- and weed-free, especially for the area you are going to sow.

METHOD It's a good idea to sow your cutting patch in straight lines, because you'll know what is supposed to be growing where, making weeding simpler. Simply pull your finger through the soil in lines, leaving 8cm between each row, so that you have a set of little trenches about 1.5cm deep. Sow your seed as thinly as possible in these trenches, cover them over using your hand or gently with a rake, and then (also gently) tamp down the soil with the end of the rake, so that there are no air pockets between seed and soil. Now water the whole thing with a fine, gentle spray. If you don't have a good watering-can rose, or hose attachment, then water the soil first, before you make your trenches.

As the seedlings come up, you'll need to thin them in stages, gently but firmly pulling out any that are growing too close together. The final distance depends on the plant. Look at the instructions on the packet and reduce the preferred distance by half.

For the other, more instantly gratifying part of your patch, look at the instructions for planting distances, reduce this by half, then plant your bought bedding in blocks or higgledy-piggledy, according to how you want your patch to look. Again, water these well, and keep any that you have left over because you may lose some plants to slugs or other things.

By autumn, you can clear everything out and plant masses of spring-flowering bulbs. Daffodils, of course, are a must and great for picking, but if you think ahead and order from a catalogue in June, you can get a wider choice. Plant these from September, but do wait until November to plant your tulips as this is thought to keep a disease called tulip fire at bay. If you plant your bulbs in straight lines, with space between each row, you can keep them there permanently and use the rows between them for planting and sowing next year's flowers. One other autumn tip is to plant some wallflowers (*Erysimum*) between your bulbs. These are available as plug plants and will give foliage over the winter months and lovely scented flowers from early spring that are perfect for cutting.

Lastly, there are two important rules to a cutting patch: the first is to be ruthless and remove anything that isn't performing as you'd like it to be, replacing it with something else; and the second is to keep cutting. Flowers will often keep on producing blooms, but only if they are prevented from setting seed, so be ready with the scissors at all times.

MORE Most of my pickings are just plonked in a vase with plain water, but if you have treasured blooms that you want to last for ages, then give them the following cocktail to drink, and this should prolong their vase life: fill your vase with equal amounts of water and lemonade (not cloudy, and not diet), then add a teaspoon of ordinary thin household bleach for every litre of liquid. The lemonade will provide sugar for the flowers and the bleach will keep the water cleaner for longer.

Turn over for pictures

Aubergines for silky, roasted yumminess

I have a thing for aubergines, probably because they soak up lots of oil without you noticing, but also because this plant has a mysteriousness to it that makes it worthy of being a nightshade family member. I love how the grow-your-own revolution has meant that we can now buy seedlings; it's a godsend for those of us who are short on time and space. This is how I like to grow aubergines.

YOU WILL NEED
An aubergine plant I love 'Black Beauty' purely because of its name and 'F1 Moneymaker' for exactly the same reason. There are lots of varieties about that are available to buy as seedlings, though.
A pot About 25cm diameter. Plastic is a good idea because you really don't want the plant to dry out. A pot saucer wouldn't go amiss, as you'll be growing the plant inside.
Multi-purpose compost I mix it with a few handfuls of John Innes No. 2 to help it retain moisture.
Tomato food Available from garden centres and usually in a red bottle.

METHOD
Plant the seedling in the middle of the pot, taking care not to damage its roots and at the same depth as it was in its previous pot. Water it in really well and place it inside a bright window-sill, so it can stay nice and warm. Ideally, you don't want night-time temperatures to fall below 21°C, but I wouldn't get too hung up on that unless you're hoping for bumper crops; much better to grow this plant for its beauty and the distinct probability that you will get two or three luscious aubergines from it.

Keep the compost moist by watering every other day or so – poking your finger into the soil at the edge of the pot will give you a good indication as to whether you need to water. As soon as you see a flower (which will be hairy and fleshy and extraordinary-looking), start feeding with the tomato fertiliser, diluted as per the instructions, at around every third watering. The flower will slowly, thrillingly, become fruit. You should pluck your aubergines when they are shiny and tight. Don't wait for them to become enormous – seize the day.

MORE
My favourite thing to do with an aubergine is to slice it up, brush it with copious amounts of olive oil, season well and roast it gently at about 150°C for 25 minutes or so, until it's golden and silky. Only on very rare occasions do such slices ever actually meet a plate, a table or another person.

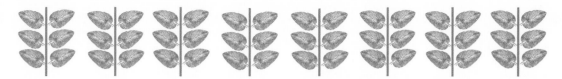

African violets – taking leaf cuttings

Velvety, gorgeous African violets are blissfully happy in the dark, dry atmosphere provided by our houses, and are therefore supremely popular with those who don't have outside space or don't want to lug massive plants about. For this reason, they seem to have acquired an unfortunate reputation (along with *Streptocarpus* and begonias) for being a sort of 'Granny plant' – and, of course, one solitary plant on top of your telly is always going to look a bit forlorn, so the trick with these is to create profusion. The Latin name for this little beauty is *Saintpaulia*. It's an evergreen perennial and it comes originally from East Africa where it grows in amongst rocks and even on tree branches. It's obvious then that this plant is not going to enjoy excessive wet, so always water it sparingly, letting it dry out completely between waterings.

A great way to increase your hoard of African violets is to take leaf cuttings, which can be done at any time during the summer. Here's how.

YOU WILL NEED

A *Saintpaulia* plant that you really love These are available in the indoor plant section of most good garden centres.

Some rooting compost I make mine out of good-quality seed compost mixed with perlite, in half-half quantities. (Perlite is a volcanic material that helps to keep things light and airy, whilst retaining moisture. It's a very good thing to use for leaf cuttings because the leaves are less likely to rot.)

A squirter with a fine spray

A few small pots I use 10cm-diameter pots.

A tray to put them on One that will fit inside your window-sill.

A clean, sharp blade I use a penknife rubbed with alcohol. A razor blade works well too, or a craft knife.

A pencil or big nail

Some sealable, clear plastic sandwich bags Or use a covered propagator.

And later

A small bag of African violet compost for re-potting Available at good garden centres. If you can't find this, then get houseplant compost.

A little pot of African violet food Available at the garden centre.

METHOD Mix up the seed compost with the perlite. Sometimes when you open a bag of perlite, there's a lot of white dust, so I always open the bag carefully and then spray water into it a few times to make it easier to handle. Now fill your little pots with the mixture, up to 5mm shy of the top, firm it down gently and place everything in a tray of water to soak for 20 minutes or so. You want the compost to be just slightly damp but definitely not sodden. The perlite will help make this less of a guessing game as it stops the mixture from getting claggy, but it also stays quite dry to the touch, so you have to see whether the bits of seed compost are dark in order to know that the water has come up to the top of the pot.

Now you need to cut your leaves. To do this, you can either remove the plant from its pot, or just gently part the rosette of leaves, and, with your sharp blade, cleanly slice through a nice, medium-sized, healthy-looking stem. Make a straight, horizontal cut, close to the base of the plant. The stalk needs to be 2–5cm long, so cut again if you need to, using a clean surface, and again make sure that the cut is clean.

Now take a pencil, or a big nail that's roughly the same thickness as the stalk, and use it to make a hole in the compost of exactly the right depth. You want the base of the leaf to be just sitting on the top of the soil. The reason for the nail or pencil is so that you don't damage the stalk as you push it into the soil. Finally, place the stalk into the hole you've made, and firm around it with your fingertips so you know it's snug. You want the soil to be in contact with the wound you've made in the stalk.

All you need to do now is put a plastic sandwich bag over each pot and seal it to keep things humid. This allows the leaf to conserve its moisture for making babies. If you're using a propagator, then you won't need a plastic bag. Repeat with more leaves if you want loads of babies and for insurance purposes (you have to be prepared for at least one of your cuttings not to make it ... that's life). Put the pots inside a window-sill that gets light, but not direct sunlight – a north- or east-facing window in a nice warm room is fine. Always water really carefully, with tepid water, either into the pot's saucer or into the pot, but making sure you don't get any water on the leaves.

Check the pots every day, making sure the compost is very slightly damp but not wet, and it's a good idea to remove the plastic bags for a few moments every other day or so to get some fresh air circulating around the plant. If all goes well, you should see some tiny leaves appearing in roughly 8–12 weeks. When you see this, remove the covering and keep nurturing them until they are large enough to handle. ('Large enough to handle' is one of those annoying gardening terms that never gets explained. It's when the leaves are large enough for a clumsy person with thick fingers to have no trouble in gently separating the baby plants from their mothers – I reckon that means 4–5cm in length.) Each leaf will produce a number of baby plantlets, each with three or four leaves and its own root system. To separate them, you need to remove the whole thing from its pot, carefully shake away the soil and pull the plantlets apart. You can now also remove the mother leaf, although I often leave it if it's difficult to separate. You need to be as gentle as possible here, creating as little root disturbance as you can.

Very carefully plant each plantlet into a new pot of the same size, filled with special African violet or houseplant compost. Continue to water carefully, and always with tepid water, letting the compost get dry to the touch between waterings. Ensure they have adequate light. Temperature-wise, African violets will be happy if you are, which is why they're such great houseplants. Start feeding every time you water, following the instructions on the pot of food. These plants come from the jungle and love high humidity, so it will make them extra-happy if you place the pots in a tray of shallow water, on top of some gravel or stones. Make sure the pots are not actually touching the water, though – they simply want the tiny droplets that will evaporate from below.

Lastly, wait until each plant is really filling its pot before you attempt to give it a bigger one, because African violets like their roots to be hugged tightly – it makes them produce more flowers.

A puff of *Nemesia* for your terrace

I clapped eyes on this wondrous thing during my first visit to the Chelsea Flower Show, where they were displayed in huge, shallow bowls, and looked like fluffy, pastel clouds of candy floss. I vowed to do the same thing at home and went straight out to find some at the garden centre. *Nemesia* come from South Africa where they hang out in scrubby places (I love this, because it means they're not too fussy). Their flowers are exquisite and, on close inspection, quite comical. They've got this frilly upper petal with four lobes like a crown, and then a lower petal that looks like a tongue sticking out. The upper and lower parts are often different colours, with a splash of yellow in the centre, which serves as a landing pad for pollinators, and sure enough, if you press down on it gently, the two bits part and you can see down the flower's throat. This is one of my summer stalwarts, prettifying my pots for months on end.

YOU WILL NEED *Nemesia* **plants** These are very popular and on sale throughout April and May in a vast array of different colours. My advice is to go and get some now in those polystyrene or plastic cells, as they will be really small and therefore cheaper.

A pot To get the puff effect, you need to go for girth, but it can be quite shallow as these are not deep-rooting plants.

Compost I use a half-and-half mixture of multi-purpose compost and John Innes No. 2 to which I often add some granular fertiliser and a few water-retaining granules if I have them to hand.

METHOD Simply half-fill your pot with compost and then gently plant the *Nemesia* at regular intervals to cover the surface. To get the close-knit cloud-like effect, I place my plants quite close together – if you've bought individual plants in cells, that means 5–7cm apart. If you've bought your *Nemesia* plants at a more mature stage, in pots, then plant each one 3cm apart. Fill in around the plants with more compost and firm everything in well. Then give the whole thing a really good soaking and wait for the magic to happen; the plants will knit together and start blooming their socks off within a couple of weeks.

The lovely thing about *Nemesia* is that it lasts for ages. Eventually, the flowers will get tall and start to flop over, and when this happens, I give the pot a haircut, snipping the whole lot to about halfway down the stems. I then give it a liquid seaweed feed and it starts flowering again after this brutal clipping.

MORE There are two other plants that I recommend for fairy-like, tiny blooms and fantastic, all-summer-long display: check out *Diascia* (a cousin of *Nemesia* and beautifully frothy in a pot); and *Verbena* x *hybrida* cultivars, floriferous and pretty in the extreme, which come in a dazzling array of different colours and habits. Some are quite prim and well-behaved, but I seem always to choose the messier, more spreading, creeping varieties which lend a wonderfully undone look to a pot.

A mass of dill

There are some herbs of which you want only a leaf or a sprig (rosemary, bay, sage); there are others you want a big bunch of (basil, coriander, parsley) – and then there is dill. My love for – and subsequent need for profusion of – this exquisitely flavoured herb is so intense that growing it from seed is an absolute necessity.

Anethum graveolens is an annual that can get really quite big, bearing umbels of bright yellow flowers above its feathery foliage. As well as being delicious, it's a thoroughly beautiful thing and I like to use it at the back of my flowerbeds to give height. Very luckily this plant needs little encouragement, and can therefore become a weed, and that's the sort of plant I love to grow. This is how you do it.

YOU WILL NEED **A packet of dill seed**

A sunny site Preferably in an area where the soil hasn't been improved with manure or soil-improvers, because dill likes things a bit tough.

METHOD You need to sow dill in the place where you want it, because it hates to be moved around. This plant will grow to an eventual height of up to 150cm, providing you with lots of leaves along the way, but it grows fast, so many people like to sow it 'successively', which means sowing new seeds every few weeks to ensure fresh leaves well into autumn. Because the plant is big, you don't need to sow lots of seed, and it's worth positioning it at the back of a border or wherever you want a tall plant.

First, prepare the soil, making sure there aren't any big lumps, then make a shallow hole in the soil with your finger or a trowel and put three seeds in it, about 5cm apart. Cover them over, water them, and I like to put a plastic cloche (see page 276) over the top to protect them from any creatures that munch. If you're planting dill as a crop in a vegetable or herb patch, then just sow a row of them. Either way, you're going to need to make sure that each plant has at least 20cm of space around it in which to grow, and that means thinning your row out when the seedlings are big enough for you to be confident about pulling them out, or, if you're growing them in specific places like me, picking the choicest of your three babies and culling the other two.

Keep the seedlings watered and a beady eye out for slugs. For plants that slugs love, I like to create a 'no-slime zone' by putting a thick circle of sharp horticultural grit around them. If you look after them, they'll start shooting up very quickly, and you may have to provide some sort of twiggy support at this point, but you can start harvesting the leaves in small amounts as soon as you're confident that the plant can take it.

When the flowers appear, its work is done and you need to cut the whole lot down, but there's no need to waste what's left of the leaves, because they freeze very well – just strip them off and put them in a plastic bag in the freezer.

MORE   My favourite thing to do with dill is to chop it up and add copious amounts of it to sour cream and blob it on fish cakes or even dunk chips in it. I couldn't possibly pick a favourite partner for it, except to say that it falls in love with anything creamy, eggy, fishy or potatoey. It is also one of the few herbal infusions that I really love.

May

My main aim with this garden is to get the 'ought to do it' stuff over with as soon as possible and then enjoy the sunshine, chewing the cud like a large, sleepy heifer. That's why, since I began on this wonderful garden-making journey, I've set myself targets to keep me focused on the main prize (namely doing as little as possible). Accordingly, I've had a mantra going in my head ever since I got here back in February, and it goes something like this:

'I will have this garden up and blooming by ... [insert name of month].'

In February, that month was March (totally sausage-esquely silly), and in March, it was April, and in April, it was the beginning of May – you get the picture. Anyway, although these milestones are always set in my head with a slight gritting of the teeth and balling of the fists, I noticed that, fabulously, my only 'labour' was in planting enough plants, and that was pretty much finished by the end of April. The rest of the 'work' was done by the plants, which filled out and started blooming in abundance as soon as they got a little sunshine in the middle of May.

We had a mini-heatwave that lasted four or five days, during which we lay on the lawn, and it really, truly did feel as if we were in a garden that had been there for years. Only the discerning would notice the small shrubs, flanked as they are by lush, bountiful mounds and spires of perennials that I planted back in March and April. The discerning would also notice that there is so much more to come, too.

I've ended up with the beginnings of a garden, and I'm planning on doing lots more to it. These things will be extra bits, like icing really, and not nearly so labour-intensive as hitherto. Summer is a time for outdoor living and enjoying friends and family, so I made May my deadline for getting the terrace cleared and full of flowering pots, ready for friends and barbecues and whatever else took my fancy.

WHAT TO DO IN YOUR VIRGIN GARDEN THIS MONTH

FILLING ANY LAST GAPS   I always, always find something wonderful that I've never laid eyes on before and just have to have. A plant that looked boring and unpromising in the shops last month may now be on your must-have list as it has burst into flower.

STAKING   This is the time to make sure that all your tall perennials, like delphiniums and poppies, have the appropriate support they need so they don't flop over and lie there looking sweet but prostrate. Support comes in a plethora of forms. You can spend money on discreet blacksmithed pieces of metal, or create a network of bamboo sticks and string, or you can use pea sticks, which are widely available in springtime. I have found these to be the prettiest and easiest solution, as all that is required is to stick them into the ground next to the plant you want to support.

ORDERING BULBS   May is the time to think about ordering your bulbs, both for summertime and autumn planting. Go online or get yourself a catalogue from a great supplier (see page 280), and order early because stocks are finite.

THE CHELSEA CHOP   The other very useful thing to do this month is to cut back your perennials for a more compact, upright shape and more flowers later in the year. This is known in gardening circles as the 'Chelsea Chop' because it is usually carried out in late May when the RHS Chelsea Flower Show is on. The theory is simple: if you cut back plants that are reaching their peak or past their best, then they will respond by putting on new growth to make more seed, and flower again in late summer. Yes, you will lose some flowering, but you'll get more flowers later, and a more compact growth habit that won't require staking.

It's impossible to give an exhaustive list of all the plants and when to chop them, but I use it to tame and bring new life to my geraniums, catmint and *Leucanthemum*, all of which form a really big part of my planting scheme. Just use your common sense and go round looking for perennials that have new growth emerging from the base. Cut these plants down to the ground, so they can regrow from the bottom. Also look for plants that have new little leaves forming from their side-shoots. Chop these ones by half, to just above the new growth. It'll be a wrench, cutting off all those lovely flowers, but fingers crossed, you'll be happy you did.

MORE WEEDING   And last but not least, keep going with the hoeing and the mowing.

Sweet cicely for sweeties

This is a seriously underrated herb. It's the first thing to appear in the garden, grows quickly and is pretty and sweet-smelling too. Its Latin name is *Myrrhis odorata* and it originally comes from southern Europe. The flowers, leaves, seeds and roots are all edible and it is so sweet that it can also be used as a sugar substitute (useful if you're trying to lose weight). The leaves have an aniseed flavour, and I made a delicious custard infused with them. I also used the leaves in a Béarnaise sauce once and it was yummy, but it's the seeds that pack the most exciting punch in terms of flavour.

You can grow sweet cicely in a pot, but it won't be happy growing in there for ever, because it's got this long tap-root which wants to explore downwards, so if you grow it in a pot, be ready to divide it when it starts to outgrow its space. For pot-culture, you'll need a mix of John Innes No. 2 and multi-purpose, and the size of your pot depends on the size of the plant you've managed to get your hands on.

YOU WILL NEED

A *Myrrhis odorata* plant This herb is becoming more popular, but it is still difficult to find in ordinary garden centres, so search for it on the internet, or better still, have a good gawp into other people's gardens and when you see it (which you will), ask them nicely if you can dig some up. They'd be very mean if they refused, as it self-seeds everywhere and many regard it as a bit of a nuisance.

A nice patch One which is moist and well-drained, and preferably with a little bit of dappled shade.

METHOD

Plant it, water it and keep watering until it's established and can fend for itself. You need do nothing more than that – it will keep coming back every year to sweeten your life.

MORE

The seeds are perfect after-dinner sweeties – honestly, just give them a try. When the flowers are over, you'll notice the seeds forming (they look like caraway seeds). Simply pick them off, or shake them from the flower umbels, and serve them in a little dish with coffee or herbal tea.

To make the custard, just scald your milk in the usual way with a couple of sweet cicely leaves added. This will be enough to flavour your sauce and have people asking what divine thing you put in it. You can use the leaves to impart sweetness in any dish. I stewed some rhubarb with half the usual amount of sugar and 3–4 chopped leaves and it worked a treat. It's a different kind of sweetness, but sweetness nonetheless.

A wisteria tree

I always used to think of wisteria as a plant unavailable to me – destined only to be a part of the lives of those lucky enough to own their own house, or a large garden. It was only when I finally got my own garden and went straight off to a wisteria nursery to buy one of these much yearned-for plants that I discovered I could have had one all along, by training it as a standard (by which I mean, made to look like a tree). I had seen wisterias in books and magazines growing like this in the middle of grand, sweeping lawns, but I never thought they could be raised to do this in a container. I should have guessed this would be the case, because wisterias are usually grown right up against the foundations of houses, which means they are shallow-rooting and therefore perfectly happy in a pot. After a long conversation with the nurseryman and wisteria expert, I came away with not one wisteria, but five (a little excessive, I know, but ho hum). A word of warning first – this project is not for the faint-hearted. It requires commitment, but then, so does having a wisteria growing up your house.

WISTERIA ABC There are four basic types, each with their own merits, but it's worth knowing a bit about them because if you're going to buy one, it'll probably be with you for life.
Wisteria brachybotrys Also known as *Wisteria venusta*. A good, vigorous wisteria, flowers in early summer.
Wisteria floribunda (Japanese wisteria) Comes in various different forms, most of which have hugely elegant, long racemes (hanging stems covered with flowers) – seriously chic, flowers in early summer. Twines clockwise.
Wisteria sinensis (Chinese wisteria) Comes in various different forms, and flowers earlier than the others. Twines anti-clockwise.
Wisteria x formosa A cross between Chinese and Japanese wisterias, this flowers early, with long racemes.

All wisteria are scented, and they come in white, purple or lilac. The best way to choose is to go to a nursery in May and see them all in flower. Always buy grafted wisteria as these are guaranteed to flower within a couple of years – otherwise you may have a long wait on your hands. Grafting is a way of propagating plants by attaching a piece of the desired plant on to a different root. In the case of wisteria, the rootstocks are raised from seed, but the top bit (the 'scion') is taken from a wisteria plant that is already flowering. The new plant behaves as if it were still a 'mature', flowering wisteria, despite being a brand-new plant. To be doubly sure of getting those flowers, choose one that is in bloom in its pot. To train a standard, try to find a single-stemmed plant.

YOU WILL NEED   **A wisteria plant** (See opposite.)

A container 40cm diameter is best, because you're going to re-pot your plant in stages. Use a plastic container for water-retention. A pot saucer is a good idea too.

John Innes No. 3 compost

A strong support You can use a bamboo cane, but know that you'll have to replace it eventually with something much stronger. A metal pole is ideal. It should be 2.5m or longer in length.

Some string

METHOD To begin with, all you need to do is plant your wisteria in the middle of the pot and replace the smaller bamboo cane that came with it with your taller one. Drive the new cane or pole carefully into the old hole so as not to damage the roots. Make sure the support goes right down to the bottom of the container so it's as secure as possible. Twine the plant up the pole in the same way it was around its old support, tie it in a couple of places, water it and leave it to grow. You may want to put your pot up against a wall, or secure it to something fixed, because the whole thing is going to be rather unstable. Make sure the container gets a good amount of sunshine – wisteria do best on south-facing walls.

If your plant is single-stemmed, it will have a main leading shoot (one tapered shoot that's taller than the others and reaching skyward). If there is more than one stem, just twine all of them round the support. It will also have quite a few more shoots like this, coming from anywhere along the stem. Keep these shoots short, no longer than 30cm long. You want to keep sap flowing into the main stem to thicken it up, and this won't happen if you remove all the side-shoots completely. When the plant has reached the height you want, pinch out the leading shoot or shoots to stop it growing upwards. This will encourage the plant to send out more side-shoots. Keep cutting the ones up the stem, but allow the shoots at the top to grow outwards.

Now the trick is to let it grow for a while and then cut the shoots at the top back by 30cm every year in the winter (January and February) so that the crown of the 'tree' starts to thicken up. Keep doing this until you've got something that looks like a tree, with a proper, gnarly trunk, and then you can start pruning in earnest, just as you would a wall-trained wisteria.

The most important thing, as always, is to water your plant. The flower buds for next year are being made between July and September this year, and a dry spell can hamper their growth, so stay vigilant with the watering can.

Here is the pruning technique, which also works for wall-trained wisterias. After flowering (so in July or August), cut back the green shoots that have just grown (I know, it's criminal isn't it?). Count five or six leaves out from the main stem and cut just above that fifth or sixth leaf. Along this whippy growth will be buds, and by cutting it, you'll encourage those buds to swell. In winter (January or February), take these same shoots and study the buds on them. Your aim is to leave two or three buds on each shoot, so cut just above the third bud. This ensures you get awesome flowers and the plant stays polite and compact. Some new, long whippy stems will have shot out after your summer pruning. Cut these back as you would for the summer pruning, except in this case you won't be guided by leaves, but by buds, so make the cut just above the fifth or sixth bud.

MORE You can of course make a standard-trained wisteria by putting it straight into the ground. A gorgeous, twisty 'tree', dripping with scented flowers in a flower border or in the middle of the lawn is my dream – all I have to do is wait a while.

Lilacs for jelly

You may be lucky enough already to have a lilac growing in your garden, but if not, then worry not one jot – lilacs are easy to grow, and you can even have them in a large container. If you don't fancy growing one, they are everywhere at this time of year, and you only need one fat flowerhead to give you the prettiest, most perfect jelly. *Syringa* are deciduous shrubs that grow almost into small trees. They are one of those plants that sit there doing not very much all year until suddenly, for a few weeks in May, they have a 'moment', rocking our world with puffy cones of hundreds of little velvety flowers which smell utterly and absolutely out of this world.

Lilacs come in loads of different colours from brightest white to deepest red, not just lilac. My favourite is *Syringa vulgaris* 'Katherine Havemeyer' which has proper lilac-coloured buds opening to lavender blue, and the blooms are 'double' which means they have lots of petals. Most importantly, they are extremely smelly – and that's the whole point. There's another one called *Syringa* x *josiflexa* which is a much smaller shrub with very beautiful, fragrant flowers, again, lavender-coloured.

YOU WILL
NEED
A lilac of which you can be proud Do a bit of trawling and find out what you want and where to get it – this plant is going to be with you for keeps if you treat it well. If you want to grow a lilac in a container, then be sure to choose a small cultivar, or even one that's been made into a standard by someone else, so you can enjoy a lovely little lollipop of blooms every year.

For growing in the ground
A generous bit of space in the garden in full sun Look at the vital statistics of your chosen cultivar – eventually it will need that amount of room to grow. Do bear in mind, though, that this is a deciduous plant, and it won't look like much over the winter, so it's a good idea to plant something evergreen next to it.
Some well-rotted manure

For growing in a container
A really large container
Some broken pieces of pot or polystyrene
John Innes No. 3 compost

METHOD Dig over your soil, incorporating a couple of spadefuls of good manure to make a nice cosy bed for your lilac, or plant it in a pot with plenty of crocks for drainage and John Innes No. 3 compost. Firm it in well and water regularly, until you can see that it's established and growing. Lilacs really don't need much looking after. It's a good idea to deadhead them when the flowers are over, so the plant can put its energy into growing rather than producing fruit. In terms of pruning though, leave the plant alone until it reaches a size and shape that suits you, and then prune it lightly after flowering, cutting just above a nice, healthy-looking bud. Once it gets old, then you can re-invigorate the plant by taking out a few entire shoots right at the base.

TO EAT You can make jelly with any edible flower, but lilacs have a special floral note to them that elevates the flavour to something truly exquisite. Just soak 3 leaves of gelatine in water, squeeze them out when they're floppy and dissolve them in half a cup of hot elderflower cordial. Over a lower heat, dissolve two tablespoons of granulated sugar into this liquid, then leave to cool. Pour in 1.5 cups of really cold prosecco, a punnet of cold raspberries and a handful of lilac flowers. Stir it all around and pour into a jelly mould. Refrigerate it for a good six hours or overnight.

MORE You can make a simple lilac syrup from the blooms too, by dissolving a cup of sugar in a cup of water, adding a handful of petals and boiling until it becomes syrup. Strain this, and you have a delicious concoction, perfect for adding to drinks, that will keep for a couple of weeks in a sealed container in the fridge.

A flowering inferno

I love using annuals that climb, mostly because I am impatient, and they are gratifyingly speedy growers, but they can also serve a useful 'filler' purpose; if you have a piece of bare wall and you're not sure what you want to plant there, you can plonk an annual in, which will clothe it beautifully for the summer whilst you do your research. I like to grow them in pots and in the ground, giving them pea sticks to scramble over, and creating an untidy, ramshackle and rather vesuvial effect (but if you want things a bit tidier, then just use bamboo canes in a wigwam). Climbing annuals are among the most lovely and useful of summer plants, and they're all over garden centres right now. There are lots of choices, but for starters, here are my favourites:

Ipomoea purpurea (morning glory) There are now many different colours but it's always 'Heavenly Blue' that captivates me.

Ipomoea lobata (sometimes known as *Mina lobata* or Spanish flag) Produces the most exquisite little 'beaks' of brightest orange fading to pale yellow.

Thunbergia alata (black-eyed Susan) A lovely plant available in yellows and oranges but always with that black 'eye' at the centre of the flower.

Cobaea scandens (cup and saucer vine) I used to grow this in my kitchen where it loved climbing slowly towards a skylight, and outdoors it is just as amazing (see overleaf). If you live in a mild area, it may stay with you as well. It's very easy to grow as it is self-clinging with wonderful tendrils that are tacky, rather than sticky.

Phaseolus coccineus (runner beans) Edible as well as gorgeous, with bright scarlet or white flowers depending on which cultivar you choose (see page 111).

YOU WILL NEED **Some small climbing plants** See my list above, but any annual that climbs is perfect. They are usually sold as seedlings in small pots at this time of year. Don't hesitate to use a combination of two different plants.

For growing in the ground
A nice area of flowerbed This must be dug over and raked.
Something for your wigwam Either bamboo canes tied with string at the top, or pea sticks given the same treatment. You can also buy metal obelisks that do the job well. You want your wigwam to be about 2 metres high.
String or garden twine
Horticultural grit

For growing in a container
A large container (and a large saucer to go underneath) 40–50cm in diameter.
A half-half mixture of multi-purpose compost and John Innes No. 2
Some water-retaining granules To mix in with the compost.
Something for your wigwam (as above)
String or garden twine

METHOD   If you're planting in the ground, assemble your wigwam and simply plant your seedlings carefully at the base of it (two at the base of each pole, and I usually put one 'inside' the wigwam and one outside). With some string or twine, tie the first little shoots in very gently to give them some direction, and water the seedlings in well, using a soft spray from the rose of a watering can. Keep a keen eye on the babies over the next couple of weeks. Seedlings like this, with their baby-soft new growth, are particularly prone to attack from slugs and snails, which is why I often put a circle of sharp horticultural grit around each one. Slimy things hate dry, sharp stuff, so they often won't cross this barrier, but even so, be vigilant.

With a container, fill it with compost and plant three or four of your little plants in the centre, spacing them evenly, but keeping them away from the very edge of the container, where you will stick your support. Make sure there's a gap of a few centimetres between the top of the compost and the lip of the container to allow for watering.

Water them in really well, standing the pot in a tray of water to make sure the compost gets a good initial soaking, and then assemble your wigwam around the edge of the pot, taking care not to spike the roots of the plants. Stand on a chair and tie some string around the top of your canes or pea sticks to bring all the ends together, and then gently tie in the bottom shoots of your plants, so they know where to start climbing. Keep watering regularly, and make sure it gets a sunny spot and you will positively see the thing growing by the second.

Whether you're growing in a pot or in the ground, keep guiding the shoots so that they eventually cover the wigwam. I often forget to do this and end up with a wonderful, massed ball of twining stems and flowers just above the top of the wigwam, which is just as beauteous, if slightly unintentional.

Turn over for pictures

Tarragon for Béarnaise sauce on a whim

I was very, very small when I was told that the way to a man's heart was through his stomach, so when I first properly fell hook, line and sinker in love with someone, I naturally tried to make myself the creator of all things delicious in his life, and this involved lots of steak Béarnaise. I've since learned that, although a man will undoubtedly fall over himself to devour a good steak, it takes rather more than that to get them to love you. But I don't regret the mistake (yes, he bolted, good and proper) because I learned how to make a Béarnaise sauce and have been relishing it ever since. This is a very long-winded way of saying that you must, if you love yourself even a little tiny bit, grow some tarragon, so that you can have it at your fingertips whenever you need it. The taste is sublime but pungent (if you grow it right), and a little goes a long way. It is also a really pretty plant, so it deserves a pot all of its own. Tarragon is a perennial which means it will die down in winter – I just hide the pot.

YOU WILL NEED   **A tarragon plant** (French, *bien sûr*, not Russian, which is bitter.) These are usually sold in 9cm pots. The Latin name is *Artemisia dracunculus*.
One pot 20cm diameter is fine for now, but be prepared to re-pot it as it gets bigger.
Compost Use multi-purpose compost with a handful of added grit to give it that 'scrubland feel'.

METHOD   Plant your little darling into its new home, making sure it's well watered and placed in a sunny spot. Keep watering it well but don't give it anything else or you'll create a slobbish, ungrateful, lazy plant that doesn't give any flavour. In midsummer, when the leaves are at their most pungent, make sure you harvest a good amount and freeze it in a labelled plastic bag or chopped, with a little water in ice-cube trays.

TO EAT   The recipe I use for Béarnaise is a simplified version of Prue Leith's classic. Put a couple of finely chopped shallots into a heavy pan with a good handful of chopped fresh tarragon leaves, four tablespoons of white wine vinegar and one teaspoon of lightly crushed peppercorns. Boil and reduce to one tablespoon of liquid, strain and leave to cool. Put this liquid into a bowl over some simmering water, along with three egg yolks and a tablespoon of water, and whisk away, adding little cubes of butter one by one, until you've whisked in almost a whole pack. Finally, add a squeeze of lemon and some more chopped tarragon leaves and eat it with steak.

A chamomile teacup

The apple scent of lawn chamomile has to be experienced to be believed. As soon as you have brushed this feathery, low-growing plant and given it a sniff, you'll understand why everyone wants a chamomile lawn, and why those who have one prize it so. I grow it in little pots outside and bring them in from time to time to put on the table for people to stroke and smell. Sometimes I nick a bit and stuff it in a teacup as a present.

Lawn chamomile, like flowering chamomile, is a hardy, evergreen perennial which means it keeps its leaves over the winter and is therefore really useful, I find, to plant with my bulbs, because it gives me something to look at and love while the bulbs are still underground. It likes a sandy soil with no big lumps or stones, and lots of sunshine. Here's how to grow it.

YOU WILL NEED

A lawn chamomile plant *Chamaemelum nobile* 'Treneague' has the strongest scent and doesn't flower. It's very popular and therefore widely available.
Compost I use John Innes No. 2 with a handful of multi-purpose to lighten it and a handful of sand.
A small pot 15cm diameter is perfect for a single plant.

METHOD

Mix the compost up really well, removing any big bits, and fill your pot with enough of it so that your chamomile plant will come to just half a centimetre below the rim. Remove the chamomile carefully from its plastic pot and plant it firmly but gently in its new pot, filling in around the sides with more compost. When you're satisfied, water the whole thing by standing it in a tray of water until the top of the compost is damp. You can of course water it from the top but as there's so little space between the top of the compost and the rim of the pot you'll be standing there for ages watering and waiting. Keep your pot in full sun and at nose height for sniffings.

MORE

If you want to display your chamomile in a teacup, simply tear off a piece, with its roots and soil, and stuff it in. Watering is a guessing game, but the nice thing about chamomile is that you can press down on it without damaging it, so you can check to see if you've over-watered by turning the cup upside down and pressing down on the plant with your fingers, squeezing out any excess water. It won't survive in here for keeps, but it's a lovely way of displaying chamomile on a table, or giving it as a gift.

Summer

June

June has been a game of two halves in my garden, first with the long-awaited roses taking centre stage, softened by a frothy chorus line of deepest azure blue geraniums. Then it all changed when the *Nicotiana* bedding, with which I covered any trace of bare earth, suddenly started singing, making the whole garden glow in the dusk. The weather calls for sunbathing and lazing around, ordering me to down tools and chill out with the dandelions on the lawn. I've stopped mowing completely, partly because I can't bear to say goodbye to the dandelions, and partly because I mowed over the power cable (oh dear) – but I tell myself that it was meant to be, because mowing is un-neighbourly on a lazy summer's day.

This is what I worked hard for at the beginning of the year; my garden has become a place for my family to enjoy, just as I wished for back in cold, dark February. The Hunk bought a fancy barbecue and friends have appeared with their children, wobbling with Jemima on squidgy, deeply creased legs and giggling in the sunshine. I've been pulling the odd weed, making sure everything is watered, and plucking off spent flowers as I walk past, but apart from that, the garden has ceased to feature on my 'to do' list, and that's just fine with me. My mistakes (and there are many) are now obligingly revealing themselves: the non-existent spires of *Verbascum* that I was so looking forward to will of course only appear next year (it is a biennial); the lack of climbing plants everywhere is irritating me too – why didn't I plant more? But these small things are fleeting – I'm still pinching myself that I have a garden at all.

Of course, my summer no-work policy means that the garden is ever-so-slightly shambolic, like a gorgeous sexy lady with bed-head, but I'm not someone who needs things pristine. Every so often I rush to rescue a tall perennial that's about to fall over, propping it up with twigs but sometimes I don't get there in time. In the lazy warmth of summer, I'm surprised by how negligent I can be – but Jemima is discovering home-grown raspberries and strawberries, eating fresh peas straight from the pod (see page 262) and has developed an incredibly sophisticated penchant for peppery nasturtiums. Apples and pears and plums are ripening, the terrace is, as I hoped, full of colourful pots and I pick a big fat bunch of sweet peas to put by my bed every single day.

WHAT TO DO IN YOUR VIRGIN GARDEN THIS MONTH

You can of course go to a garden centre and buy bulbs for planting in the autumn, but you'll get a far wider choice and better bulbs if you order them from great growers right now. Don't be mean (I didn't order nearly enough bulbs and had to go out and buy more in the shops when the time for planting came). See page 280 for a list of suppliers, and do take advice from these people – they are experts and full of good recommendations. I can't list all my favourite bulbs because it would take up the whole of this book, but do make sure you have each of the following, all of which will be despatched to you around September time:

Allium (Tall stalks with purple pompoms on top – see opposite)
Tulipa
Camassia (White or blue with loads of delicate, star-like flowers)
Iris
Corydalis (Low-growing with delicate leaves and long, tubular flowers of yellow, blue or lilac)
Fritillaria meleagris (snakeshead fritillaries – chequered, nodding beauties in white or purple)
Hyacinthoides non-scripta (English bluebells)

Also, it's worth ordering prepared hyacinths for flowering indoors over the winter (see page 174) and *Colchicum* (naked ladies – big crocuses with white stems) – both of which will be despatched in the summer.

I learned to love my shaggy lawn because my mower broke, but if you like things ordered, and can manage only one 'job', then make it mowing the lawn. Mind-numbingly dull it may be, but in terms of transformation, mowing really pays you back for your work in a way that no other gardening job will, making you feel like your garden is tidy and calm and under control.

Gladiolus callianthus for sultry scent

Some of the best things in life are just fluke, and this is one of them. I picked up a packet of these corms on a whim when I first began dabbling with plants. I was attracted to the picture on the packet – those milky-white, lily-like blooms with that sexy, dark purple blotch in the centre – but I had no idea how deeply delicious the flowers would smell. I planted them, following the sparse instructions on the label; and they bloomed perfectly, pumping out their alluring scent (which is darker and more mysterious than anything you can buy in a bottle). I have been growing them every year since, in ever larger numbers, and always in pots. They flower in late summer and early autumn, which is the perfect time to have something clean and white and gorgeous-looking. They're not hardy, and I don't go in for lifting and storing bulbs (well, not yet anyway), so I tend to start afresh with new corms each year. Here's how I grow them.

YOU WILL NEED *Gladiolus callianthus* **corms** As many as you have pots for (see below). Available to buy online and in good nurseries. Often sold under their old name *Acidanthera*.
Compost I use two-thirds ordinary peat-free multi-purpose mixed with one-third John Innes No. 1 or 2 to give it some weight and stability.
Pots I tend to use tall long-tom type pots as these are tall, graceful plants. Mine are mostly 25cm diameter by 30cm height, but if you don't have long toms they work fine in regular pots too – just make sure any pot is at least 25cm deep.

METHOD Mix your compost and then fill your pot to 13cm from the top. I usually put seven corms in a 25cm diameter pot. Space them evenly with the pointy bit upward and then cover them with 10cm more compost, patting down gently. This should leave you with a 3cm gap between the top of the compost and the rim of the pot for efficient watering. Now just water your pot thoroughly, until you can see water draining out of the hole at the bottom. Place the pot somewhere warm and sunny, and keep it watered, and you'll get show-stopping flowers within a few weeks. The scent is the main event here, so put them somewhere with regular human traffic – people will literally stop and sniff the air.

MORE You can plant corms in April and May too for slightly earlier flowers. A few pots of these, placed strategically in your flowerbeds (you can even dig holes for the pots if you like) make the ultimate gap-filler for late summer and autumn chic.

A *Verbena* screen

I am always searching for new ways to give height to my garden, whether that is on my terrace or in the borders, and that's why I love to grow foxgloves, delphiniums, *Verbascum* and annual climbers crawling over wigwams. But there are times when something altogether more delicate is called for, something so ethereal that it is almost see-through, and that is when I turn to this plant. Tall, strong, thin stems are topped with tiny, purple flowers that bob about in the breeze (see overleaf). They provide interest at eye-height, and a sort of screen that is both there and not there. Now I have it dotted through the borders, but in my balcony days it would shoot up every summer from pots that I had forgotten it inhabited. I would line these up to create a diaphanous screen and often bring them indoors to create 'walls' in my one-room flat.

    Verbena bonariensis comes from a huge genus full of pretty flowers, many of which are perfect for summer bedding and container gardening (see page 87). This one is a perennial and is frost hardy, coming as it does from South America, Brazil and Argentina. That means that it'll do fine in most areas, unless you live very far north. It will come back year after year, and spread itself about if it's happy, and will clump up obligingly so that you'll be able to divide your plants and get more eventually. The other really important thing about this plant is that the bees love it.

YOU WILL NEED   **At least 6 *Verbena bonariensis* plants** You can grow it from seed (and this is much more economical than buying it ready-grown), but I have a hard time getting it to germinate, so I have stipulated bought plants in the spirit of instant gratification.

For growing in a container
6 containers of your choice or a couple of deep window-boxes Obviously these need to have drainage holes.
Crocks Polystyrene is best but broken pottery is fine too.
John Innes No. 2 compost
Multi-purpose compost
Fertiliser granules
Horticultural grit
Some white lobelia or something else to under-plant with (Optional.)

For growing in the ground
A sunny site in the garden

METHOD   Put a layer of crocks at the bottom of each container (I use crocks here because John Innes compost is very heavy and it can block the holes at the bottom of containers if you're not careful). Fill your containers up to where the base of the plant will sit with three-quarters John Innes No. 2, one-quarter multi-purpose compost, fertiliser granules as per instructions on the packet, and a couple of handfuls of horticultural grit. Make sure your plants are watered well and plant them carefully at the same level as they were in their plastic pot, leaving 3cm clear at the top of the pot for watering. If you're under-planting, then put the lobelia, or whatever you're using, around the edge, spacing as per the label on their packet. Water the containers well, place them where you want them, and wait for the wafty, bobbing flowers to appear in a few weeks.

If you're not using containers, select a sunny site, dig a hole and plant your *Verbena* firmly. Don't be limited by thinking this tall beauty has to go at the back of your flowerbed – it is both diaphanous and self-supporting, so it won't block the view.

The pots or window-boxes can create different spaces in the garden. They also make a fantastic, romantic walkway, or a temporary screen where you are thinking of putting a hedge; the possibilities for a moveable, beautiful 'wall' are manifold.

MORE   These beauties will die down over the winter, and you can either put the pots somewhere frost-free and wait until they reappear, watering very sparingly over the cold months, or carefully plant something else around the edge, like small trailing ivy, or little tulip bulbs to come up in spring.

Eventually, you'll need to remove your plants from their containers and divide them up because they'll be getting squashed. Do this in spring and, making sure your plant is well watered beforehand, simply remove the entire thing from its pot, lay it on the ground and brutally chop it into quarters with a sharp spade. Your screen will be four times as long now (or you can start giving plants away to lucky friends).

Turn over for pictures

Trailing beauty

Being a pot and hanging basket gardener at heart, there is one trailing plant (apart from ivy) that I use again and again. More often than not, I'm a 'just green' kind of a person, which is why this plant – which is normally used in conjunction with brightly coloured flowers – always gets its own container in my space.

Glechoma hederacea 'Variegata' (known pretty much universally as trailing nepeta) is a woodland ground ivy with softly variegated, scalloped leaves. It's a perennial and semi-evergreen, which means it gives a really lovely, long growing season. It's happy living in containers or window-boxes and grows at a rate of knots. You can find it as tiny plugs early in the season, or in small pots over the summer months. The year I discovered *Glechoma,* I had to give over my whole balcony to it for a good few months – it was just so beautiful that I didn't need or want anything else. This recipe is for one hanging basket, but you'll want more.

YOU WILL NEED

Glechoma plants The number will depend on the size of the plants and your basket, but I like to plant them 10–15cm apart.

1 hanging basket of your choice The bigger the better.

Compost I use a half-and-half mixture of peat-free multi-purpose and John Innes No. 2.

Fertiliser granules

Water-retaining granules

METHOD Water your plants first, and then mix your compost with the fertiliser and water-retaining granules, following the instructions on the packets for amounts. Now fill your basket to about 10cm from the top and water the whole thing so that the water-retaining granules can expand, otherwise they'll push your plants out of the basket.

After about an hour it's safe to plant, so make some little holes in the compost around the edge of the basket and squidge the *Glechoma* plants into place, adding more compost if necessary. I don't normally plant any in the middle unless I'm doing a huge basket because I like to hang them well above head-height (it's all about the trailing leaves), and the more room there is for the roots, the better.

Finally, water the whole thing well and hang it up high. Water it carefully and regularly and you'll be walking through a forest of delicately scalloped, tickling tendrils in no time. At the end of the season, when things begin to look a bit tatty, you can cut it back, plant something else in with it, and wait for it to reappear the next year.

MORE There are two other trailing beauties which deserve a mention here, and require the same treatment. The only difference with these two is that they need replacing with new plants the following year.

Dichondra argentea 'Silver Falls' has delicate, silvery, velvet leaves. It is an evergreen perennial in non-frosty areas, so here in the UK it tends to be treated like an annual. It grows really fast, daintily covering huge areas of bare earth and sending out long shoots which hang over the sides of a container.

Helichrysum petiolare is a soft, woolly-leaved evergreen shrub that is sensitive to frost, so like *Dichondra*, it's often treated here as an annual. Although the stems are quite tough and therefore don't 'hang' like the other two, it still trails prettily, albeit in a more horizontal fashion. There are various cultivars around, some with yellow leaves, some miniature, but the silvery, pale green loveliness of the original is hard to beat.

Pot-pourri – the rosy way

When I was a little girl there was an explosion of interest in pot-pourri – it was everywhere, often sold in plastic bags and mainly consisting of coloured wood chips and a few flower heads with any number of little scent bottles that you were supposed to dribble on to it at regular intervals to keep the scent strong. Wrong wrong wrong, because pot-pourri is supposed to be smelly in itself. You can of course add essential oils to prolong the scent, but if you keep the pot-pourri in a bowl with a lid, then you'll get a good few weeks' worth of scent – after which you can use the darling little buds to decorate a cake, or a present, or float in your bath.

You can use any scented flower for pot-pourri, but I stick to roses. This is because I can't resist picking them, and often there are tiny buds on the spray that will never open in water. When the main roses are over, I just cut them off and use the little ones for drying ... waste not, want not.

YOU WILL NEED

Some rosebuds From a scented rose, naturally.
A ball of string
Somewhere cool, dry and dark
Some scissors or sharp secateurs
A shallow bowl Preferably one with some sort of covering.

METHOD

First, you need to gather your blooms. Pick them in tight bud, well before they open, in sprays, so that you'll be able simply to hook them over your string (see below). If you want to use pre-cut flowers that you've been given, then it's fine to dry them after you've displayed them for a while.

To dry them, you need to make a washing line by attaching a length of string somewhere dark and out of the way. I use my basement, but the back of a cupboard would work – just make sure there's no humidity. Hook the sprays over this line of string so they're upside down, and then leave them alone, or lay individual blooms on a tray lined with absorbent kitchen paper, making sure they don't touch each other. The place will start smelling wonderful as the buds dry. After a couple of weeks, they should be completely dry, so snip them off very close to the base of each flower and topple the whole lot into a bowl. That's your rosebud pot-pourri.

A flower for your hair

A real flower in your hair is the absolute epitome of nonchalant beauty. It's all very well picking a gorgeous bloom and offering it up to your tresses, but getting it to stay there is another matter. Here is a simple way of getting the job done, with no wires or pliers or special equipment in sight. It comes courtesy of the deeply fabulous Miss Pickering whose eponymous blog is a constant source of inspiration.

YOU WILL NEED **A freshly plucked bloom that you love** Any will do, but perhaps something robust, like a rose, rather than something ephemeral, like a poppy.
A safety pin
A hair grip the same colour as your hair

METHOD Cut the flower stalk right up at the top, leaving enough at the base of the flower for the pin to go in to. Now, drive your safety pin through the base of the flower, close it up and slip the hair grip through the closed safety pin.

Stick the whole thing into your hair, hiding the hair grip and the safety pin within your gorgeous tresses.

And there you have it – a flower you can wear that won't fall out. You should now probably put on a wafty dress and find a festival, sharpish.

A year-round window-box

A glorious, bursting window-box is not just about 'curb appeal' (although, having searched for property, I can see how dead, crispy window-box flowers might lead to one house being valued less than its blooming neighbour). The point of a window-box is to please not just passers-by, but yourself. You're the one who sees the damn thing every day, from the inside as well as outside. You're the one who waters it – it's yours, so love it, and while you're at it, why not make the whole thing easy.

   This is my recipe for a window-box that you only have to make up once. You fill it mainly with plants that look good all year round, and then you fill the gaps with temporary plants as often as you please. Once it's made up, changing the plants is easy because you've done a naughty little trick (see below), which means you don't even have to get your hands dirty. I suggest you begin your window-box now, at the beginning of summer, because that will give the trailing evergreens enough time to grow and be gorgeous when they're really needed in winter. But, actually, you can do this at any time of the year. Likewise, aspect (which way your window-box faces) has little relevance here, as most of the planting is evergreen.

YOU WILL NEED **A window-box** The type of box depends obviously on your taste and budget, but I would make a gentle plea here for plastic over terracotta. I know the idea of a plastic window-box is sort of hideous, but it is much slower to dry out, and therefore easier on you. Try to find something at least 20cm deep, possibly more. The quantities of evergreens here are for any size window-box between 50cm and 1 metre.

Compost A half-and-half mixture of John Innes No. 2 and multi-purpose compost.

Water-retaining gel granules

Fertiliser granules

Crocks Broken bits of polystyrene are best.

1 evergreen plant that's been clipped or topiarised into a fairly compact, smart shape A little ball or cone of box, widely available and sold in a 20cm diameter pot is always a winner. Bay clipped into a cone shape is beautiful, as well as useful as you can cook with it, or you could go for a more relaxed look and use rosemary or lavender (see instructions for pruning lavender on page 171). You need something central and solid to make it look substantial as well as smart.

2 tiny pots of small ivy These are widely available in pots at the garden centre; pick something dainty and unusual.

2 medium-sized pots of Mexican daisies (*Erigeron karvinskianus*) The perfect plant, in my opinion, and once you've finished with it, you can plant it out in the garden. You could also use *Verbena*, *Pelargonium* (geraniums), or forget-me-nots. This is your main flowering plant, and you want something pretty and cloud-like to fill the space.
2 small pots of *Nemesia* or pansies Something contrasting in colour and lower-growing than your main flowers (optional).
1 small pot of *Bacopa*, *Dichondra* or *Helichrysum* To trail down the front of your box.
1 pack of bedding petunias These are sold in polystyrene cells and in lots of different hues to suit your colour scheme. They are perfect for squidging into the gaps of your box.
A pair of sharp scissors

METHOD Before you do anything, make sure your window-boxes fit properly on your window-sill and that there is no chance of them falling off. If you're even the slightest bit worried, then fix a bracket or two on to the sill so you can sleep at night. Also, it's vital that your box has drainage, so if it comes with holes in the bottom, then great, but if not, you'll need to drill some.

Ensure that all your plants are well-watered, and then mix your compost in a big trug. You need to add fertiliser granules and water-retaining gel in the quantities stipulated on the packets. Make sure everything is mixed really well and then scatter a layer of polystyrene at the bottom of the box and fill it up halfway with compost.

Now remove your evergreen from its plastic pot and plant it bang in the centre and at the back, so it's touching the edge of the box. Plant it at the same level it was in its previous pot, and at a depth that ensures there is a good three or four centimetres between the top of the compost and the rim of the box.

Next, do the same with your ivy, planting them in the two front corners of the box (you will have to put more compost into the box so that the ivy is planted at the right level). Now for the clever bit – all your other plants, apart from the petunias, are going to stay in their plastic pots, but first you are going to cut the bottoms off them. To do this, remove the plants from their pots and carefully set aside. Take a pair of sharp scissors and cut the bottom of each pot clean off, so you're left with a tube. Replace the plant in its tube and plant it in your box. Do this exactly as you please (the design is supposed to be symmetrical, which would mean your daisies and your *Nemesia* either side of your evergreen, with the *Bacopa* in the centre at the front – but, hey, this is your window-box).

This will all be a little messy because you want to make sure there are no gaps and that everything, including the sides of the box and the plants in their pots, is filled with compost. This means positioning the plants where you want them, holding them in place with one hand and squidging compost into the gaps with the other. It takes a bit longer than you think, but eventually you will end up with everything at the same level, and a thin layer of compost covering the tops of the plastic pots so they're out of sight. Don't worry about squeezing the roots of the plants a bit to get them into their places – they'll be fine as long as you don't break too many of them.

SUMMER

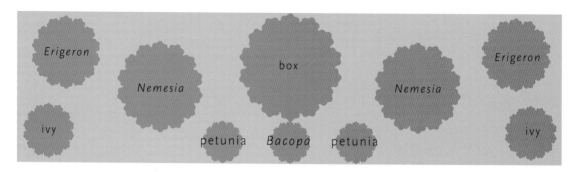

AUTUMN

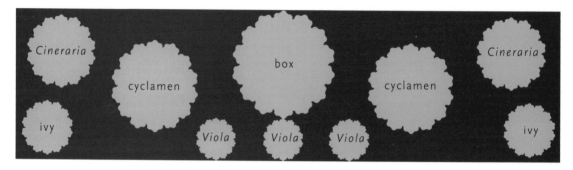

WINTER

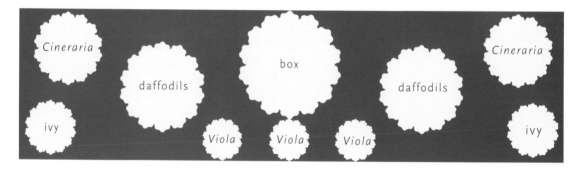

SPRING

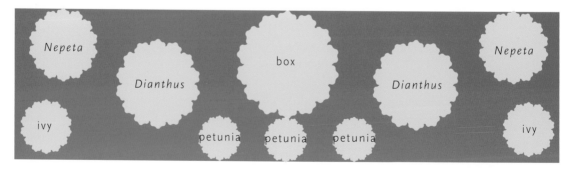

Depending on the size of your window-box, there will now be either teeny-weeny gaps around the edges, or rather larger ones. Carefully remove your petunias one by one from their cells (be very careful, because they are rather brittle) and squish them into these gaps so that every available space is filled.

All that remains is to water your window-box thoroughly, by which I mean put it in a tray and water it gently over the top until you see water coming out of the bottom. Leave it in the tray full of water for a couple of hours to make sure it's soaked, and then put it on your window-sill.

The magic is that when the temporary plants in their pots die down or start boring you to death, you can change them quickly and instantly for another plant that you love.

MORE **An autumn window-box**

In September, replace the daisies with *Cineraria maritima* (a beautiful plant with silver foliage and widely available), and the *Nemesia* with cyclamen (these come in white and all the reds you can imagine, but for autumn I love deep, saturated pink). Just remove the plants from their plastic and plonk them in the empty, bottomless pot that's already buried in the window-box. Pull out the petunias carefully, and the *Bacopa* too if you are tired of it, and replace with plugs of *Viola* (I like fiery yellows and oranges for this time of year), and sprinkle a little more compost in any gaps. Water it well, and be smug because it took you so little time.

A winter window-box

In December, replace the cyclamen with two little pots of miniature daffodils – they are everywhere in the garden centres right now, with pale green spears peeping up out of the soil. I love them because they remind me of spring when everything is bleak, but if you want something more festive, use little pots of skimmia or cyclamen again, but this time in red or white. December is a busy time, so don't do anything else – the *Cineraria* will beautifully and obligingly take you through the winter, as will the *Viola*. Add more compost to fill in any gaps and water everything in really well.

A spring window-box

In March, replace the *Cineraria* with little pots of *Nepeta* x *mussinii* – a lovely, aromatic plant that I use in the garden as a relaxed, low hedge. You can plant it out in the garden when you've finished with it. At this time of year, the garden centres are full of small pots of perennials so it's a great idea to take advantage of that and buy something you can plant out in the garden when it outgrows the space. Obviously, not everything will fit the bill – your plant has to be happy in a window-box for three months, so there's no point going for anything too tall like a lupin or a delphinium. Read the labels for eventual height and spread, and you'll get an idea of what's possible.

Replace the daffodils with two small pots of *Dianthus* (garden pinks). I like red or pink, because by March we still have Easter to come, and I'm hankering for something

not yellow. Finally, remove the *Violas* which have done you such long service, and replace them with some early-flowering petunias (again, look at the labels to find out flowering times). Fill in again with a little more compost and water well.

Other suggestions for your spring window-box are *Stachys, Primula, Alchemilla, Heuchera* and any herbs. It is also best to steer clear of spring bulbs because they won't last until June.

Here are my window-boxes in their first year, using the methods above. Top row, left to right: summer and autumn. Bottom row, left to right: winter and spring.

AND ONE MORE THING If you have box topiary in your window-box, clip them in May or June, and again in August or September to keep a really neat shape (see Slow topiary on page 194). Bay needs clipping too (at the same times), but try to remove whole leaves to keep the shape, rather than cutting them in half, which just looks weird. If you've got lavender in your box, follow the pruning regime on page 171.

In subsequent years, it's a good idea to feed your evergreens in the springtime by removing the top layer of compost directly around the plant and replacing it with new.

July

Imagine a party in full swing, with everyone roaring drunk and falling over. My no-work-while-the-sun-shines ethos has meant that the garden is rather grandly Havisham-esque. It's now, in high summer, that plants begin to 'turn' and more yellows and oranges start to enter the fray. This first summer is proving truly fruitful; long runner beans hang from tripods, and apples, pears and tomatoes are swelling enticingly. There is not even the tiniest gap in the flowerbeds; a billowing sea of colour with tall verbenas (see page 124), honesty and great fat swords of blue delphiniums swaying over everything. In amongst the crowded blooms, there are lilies, still tightly shut but promising to burst soon.

Now, at this high point for flowers, I realise that when they are all a distant memory, I'm going to want more evergreen structure to carry me through the winter months. Instant gratification will have to wait (because I am stony-broke right now), but I am still poised for a blow-out on box balls and some little bay trees or holly trees to put in the flowerbeds very soon. In the meantime, I resolve to start growing and clipping my own box topiary (see page 194). It's a long game, but a satisfying, money-saving one.

Mr Pug has made himself ill by gorging on fallen plums; nevertheless, the memory of how delicious they were overrode everything in his diminutive brain and he has been obsessed with the plum tree ever since, gazing mournfully up into the branches for hours on end. I am busy collecting bunch after bunch of sweet peas, mixed with pinks (*Dianthus*), acid-green lady's mantle (*Alchemilla mollis*) and retina-burning pink *Lychnis coronaria*. My little cutting patch is yielding huge amounts of bubblegum-scented snapdragons (*Antirrhinum*), delicate, sweet-smelling stocks (*Matthiola longipetala*), and frothy *Ammi majus*. The lavender is doing its fabulous thing – looking, smelling and sounding wonderful (lavender in flower is always covered in buzzing bees), but its flowers are almost over, so I'm chopping it back in order to get the best shape and blooms next year (see page 142).

When I walk out into the garden I find it hard to believe it is only six months old, but on the terrace, everything is getting a bit floppy, and whilst that's fine in the flowerbeds, I've been giving my pots a haircut in the hope that they'll give me a second flush of flowers for late summer. It's always a bit scary doing this, and everything looks a bit like a child whose sibling has decided to play hairdresser for the day. I tend to hide these pots away while they put on a bit of growth, so they have been replaced by tomatoes in pots, *Nicotiana* and a mass of pelargoniums that are blooming as if every moment were their last.

WHAT TO DO IN YOUR VIRGIN GARDEN THIS MONTH

LOOKING AT STRUCTURE
July is an odd time in the garden centre where there's a real lull in terms of inspiration. It's that turning point where you get lots of old and rather tired-looking bedding plants that haven't been sold yet, and it all makes you feel that you can't bear to look at another lobelia. Soon the late-summer flowers will start to appear and everything will seem okay again, but in the meantime, if you feel the urge to shop, then turn your attention to what looks great all year round. Think about whether you've got enough winter wonder in your planting scheme – when all the fluff is stripped away, have you got green stuff to make things feel less bare? If not, then now is the time to snap up a bit of box or yew or something evergreen to create what garden designers call 'structure' or 'bones'. As long as you make sure they are really well watered for a few weeks after planting, then it's fine to get them in the ground right now, ready to shine for autumn.

LOOKING OVER THE FENCE
This is also the perfect time to get nosy and note down what you love about other people's gardens. For me this usually means herbaceous perennials that I forgot to get in the spring. *Anemone* x *hybrida*, *Gaura lindheimeri*, *Phlox paniculata* and *Astrantia major* are all plants I'll be looking to get my hands on. If money is tight, then buy just one and get it in the ground. You'll be able to divide most perennials ad infinitum next spring (see page 33), and take root cuttings of others in November (see Root cuttings for clouds of anemone on page 208), so there's no need to spend a fortune.

CHOPPING LAVENDER
If you've put lavender in your garden, whether in a pot or in the ground, chop off the flowers when they're past their best. This will make the plant concentrate its energy into roots and shoots and is the first stage of a lavender pruning programme that will have you chopping them back quite drastically at the end of September (see page 171) in order to get wonderful bushy, ball-like shrubs that will flower their socks off next year.

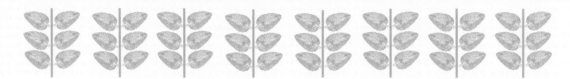

Santolina for keeping moths at bay

Santolina (or cotton lavender) is a Mediterranean plant that looks great as an informal low hedge, in place of lavender or even box. It's evergreen (or, at least, evergrey) and bears pretty little, yellow pompom flowers in the summer. The other lovely thing about it is its aromatic foliage, which (I read) will deter moths, and I haven't seen any new holes in my clothes since I started using these moth bags. *Santolina* looks particularly gorgeous in terracotta pots and that is what I have specified here, but you can of course grow it in the ground (see below).

YOU WILL
NEED

1 *Santolina* plant – there are a few different varieties out there, but for me the loveliest is plain old *Santolina chamaecyparissus* with bright yellow flowers.

For growing in a container
1 terracotta pot 40cm diameter should be fine for now.
Multi-purpose compost with a few handfuls of added horticultural grit The grit gives extra drainage and adds paucity to the soil. If this plant gets too many rich pickings it will lose its colour and vigour.

For growing in the ground
A sunny site Make sure that it has great drainage and not too much richness – add sand or grit to your soil if it's too posh.

METHOD

Plant the *Santolina* in the centre of your pot, at the same depth that it was in its original container, and water it in well. It needs to be placed in a sunny spot and should fill out quickly (its natural spread is about a metre).

If you're planting in the ground, make sure your site is in full sun. If you want a hedge, then space the plants 30cm apart, and you'll need to clip it regularly in the spring and summer if you want it to keep its shape. That means you'll have to forgo the flowers but you can always plant some others elsewhere for those golden pompoms.

To make moth sachets (which make lovely presents), just harvest some of the foliage and put it somewhere warm to dry out for about a week; I tie some string to a radiator and hook each sprig over it. When the leaves are dry, crush them between your fingers and fill muslin squares with the brittle slivers, tying them with ribbons. If you want the sachet to smell extra yum, then add dried, crushed rosemary, mint, or both.

A herb box for movers

I empathise keenly with anyone enduring the pain of moving house, and one of my very first acts of gardening when we arrived here back in February was to sow some basil seeds (see page 256), both to calm me down, and to remind me that summer wasn't far away. With the weather warmer, and the shops full of young plants, it's wonderfully easy to assemble the perfect housewarming present: a herb garden in a box.

YOU WILL NEED

A six-pack of herbs from the garden centre You can get these in pre-made packs, containing a set of essential herbs, or just choose the ones you love the most. The number of pots depends on their size, and on the size of your box. I usually try to get in as many flavours and textures as possible. This box (see opposite) contains oregano, chives, thyme, basil, sage and parsley.

A wooden box that looks lovely I beg mine from wine merchants who would otherwise throw them out.

A drill with a drill bit for wood

A large, strong plastic bag to line your box (Optional.) I rather lazily don't bother doing this as it's a temporary herb garden and all the plants will hopefully be used up anyway. Lining the box will keep it from warping and eventually falling apart, so that it can be used again. If you are lining your box, you'll also need a heavy-duty staple gun to attach the plastic sheet to the inside of the box.

Some pieces of polystyrene or broken pieces of terracotta pot

Compost Mix half-and-half multi-purpose compost with John Innes No. 2. (You could just use multi-purpose, but it's very bad at retaining water, and movers are busy people. A bit of John Innes No. 2 will ensure the herbs stand a fighting chance of survival if someone forgets to water them for a day or three.)

A big ribbon to tie round the whole thing

METHOD

First you need to drill some big holes in the bottom of your box – six should do it. This allows the water to drain away so the compost doesn't get too soggy. Remember that most herbs come from the Mediterranean where it's definitely *not* soggy. If you're lining your box, then cut a large piece of plastic and put it inside the box, squishing it into all the corners. Roll the edges under and staple them so that the top of the plastic lies just shy of the top of the box – you mustn't be able to see it from the outside. Now cut a few holes in the plastic at the bottom, so that the water can get out of the holes you have drilled in the wood.

Put a layer of polystyrene pieces at the bottom of the box and fill it up halfway with compost. Take your herbs out of their plastic pots and arrange them in the box, filling in around the edges with more compost. Push down firmly, adding more compost if you are left with any gaps. Put the whole box in a tray or something similar, and water it until you see water coming out of the holes at the bottom. Water some more, until the tray is filled and the whole box is sitting in a shallow pool of water. Leave it there for a few hours to make sure that all the compost is fully watered. Remove it from the tray, allow it to dry and then tie a bow around the box, and go round to delight your friends with it. Note: a bit of chocolate wouldn't go amiss here either.

A simple summer wedding bouquet

The more I mess around with garden-grown flowers, the more I wish I could get married all over again and have the flowers of my dreams. The reality is, though, that only the most chilled-out of brides has the time or inclination to make their own bouquet. No, this is something to do for your sister or your best friend. It really is just a posy, but made with bombastic amounts of love and care, and observing a few extra rules. I'm no florist, but this is something that anybody could do – all that is required is to know and love your bride, to have some inkling of what's pretty, and to bear the following in mind.

First, the bouquet has to be strong enough to take a bit of a battering. This means it needs to be really securely tied and all the stalks have to be long enough to be a part of the main 'stem' of the bouquet. I'm often guilty of tying a posy and then adding bits to it by pushing stems into the head of flowers. This won't do for a wedding.

Second, if you're using lilies or anything with large pollen-loaded anthers, you're going to need to take extra care and snip them off during conditioning (see below).

YOU WILL NEED **A selection of snippings from the garden** I used *Ammi majus*, *Rosa* 'Winchester Cathedral' (a white, scented rose), *Lathyrus odoratus* (sweet pea) – a white, scented one, *Nepeta* (catmint) for a bit of blue, and *Astrantia major* – a pink one for a bit of blush.
Sharp secateurs
Sharp scissors
Vases full of water
Some heavy-duty gardening gloves
A mirror
A length of buff-coloured garden string about 40cm long
Ribbon or lace for tying your bouquet in a colour that your bride will adore

METHOD Pick your flowers and foliage with as much stalk as you can and then put them straight in water. 'Condition' the stems, which means fussing around with each stem until it's perfect, removing at least half of the leaves from the bottom of the stem upwards, and then any other foliage that's at all manky, ensuring there are no little bugs crawling around, etc. You should end up with a vase of flowers on long stems with a few leaves at the top. With roses, remove all the thorns from the stems by putting on some thick gardening gloves, gripping each stem and rubbing it until all the thorns are stripped.

Now it's time to get creative. Imagine you're the bride and stand in front of a mirror as you build the posy. I don't know how the proper florists do this, but I start with one large-ish flower, like a rose, hold it in one hand, and work around it by adding different stems until I have a nice bunch. I keep checking the posy in the mirror, and I keep rotating it by swapping it from my left hand to my right and back again in order to add more flowers on each side. You want to end up with something that the bride can pick up any which way, and it looks magical. The only exception to this is if you're adding a trailing element, in which case your posy will have a 'this way up' thing going on, with the trailing bits at the bottom. I always keep a firm grip on the stems and try not to fiddle with anything once it's in (if there is something in the middle you don't like, then it's better to snip it off altogether than try to remove it). You'll be doing quite a bit of conditioning as you go, snipping off bits of leaf that you don't need, and separating sprays of flowers. This will happen more and more as you reach the outside, because you'll want shorter-stemmed, smaller sprays of flowers around the edge, which then tumble down over the bride's fingers, just above the ribbon.

Once you're generally happy (and don't worry, because you can always add more), take your length of string and lay it over your stems, near the top, but not too close to the flowers, holding the middle of the string in place with your thumb, winding one end tightly around the stems a couple of times, and then repeating with the other end, going the other way around. When you've done this, your flowers should be bound tightly enough for you to let go of the stems and tie the string in a knot. The reason you don't want the string too high up is that you eventually want it hidden by your ribbon. Now cut your stems so they're all the same length with a pair of good secateurs. Make sure you leave the bride enough to grip on to, though.

Put the whole thing in a glass of water and decide whether you want to add more around the edges, in which case you'll need to repeat the tying process with more string over the top of what you've just done. If you're satisfied, then leave it in water in a cold room until you're about to take it to the bride, at which point you should tie it up with the prettiest bow or knot imaginable. If you've chosen lace, or a trimming that won't show damp, then you can do this well beforehand and have it sitting in water. If possible, try to keep the thing in water up to the last half-hour or so, and don't forget to have paper towel ready to dry off the stems before you hand over your creation to the bride.

Turn over for pictures

APRIL. 18" HIGH
£3·80 FOR 10 £36·00 100
TRIUMPH TULIP
ARABIAN MYSTRY
MAY 20" HIGH
£3·20 FOR 10 £30·00 100
GREAT FOR BEDDING.
TRIUMPH TULIP
YELLOW LIGHT

August

August is a funny old month in the garden. Whatever the weather, it's always a time of transition. It doesn't seem to matter how much care and attention is lavished on a plot, the August garden always looks a little spent – like someone with a bit of a hangover. It's hardly surprising that things seem this way, as we can't resist looking back to the glory that was June and July, whilst looking forward to the cosy mellowness of the autumn and winter, and poor old August is stuck there in the middle. When I lived in a flat and grew all my plants in pots on a balcony, this 'August hangover' was less apparent. When things started to go brown, or fall over, or didn't look lovely any more, I'd just move that pot to somewhere less noticeable or plant something else in it – but things are different in a garden. There's a certain ennui, a slight dissatisfaction, that faintly uncomfortable 'too-much-of-a-good-thing' feeling that makes you sigh and wish something would radically change.

The only way around this rather Chekhovian state of affairs is to watch what's going on in the garden, notice what a great time the birds and the bugs and the frogs are having, and learn to love it. Flowers are going to seed, producing an entirely different look, and colours are fading slowly so that there are fewer clear blues and more reds and browns. But seedheads are essential both for your garden's future beauty and for many birds and insects who rely on them for food, so don't cut them down unless they're absolutely driving you bananas. In the second week of August, I grabbed my secateurs and did a general garden tidy-up, getting rid of spent flowers and cutting back anything that had fallen over. As a result of this, by the end of the month, my hardy geraniums, *Alchemilla mollis* (lady's mantle) and various other plants had started flowering again. I also removed a few plants that were crowding and squashing their neighbours. Consequently, everything has room to breathe, and I've also got some space to plant all the bulbs that will arrive soon.

The roses that gave me so much in June have decided to return for an encore with absolutely no help or encouragement from me. They're not as huge and sumptuous as they were, but they're gorgeous nonetheless. I have been making large amounts of ice-cream with my favourite herb, lemon verbena, which doesn't survive the winter outdoors. This urge to preserve has had me filling the whole freezer, but luckily we all love ice-cream (particularly the Hunk). I continue to ransack the cutting patch with zeal, and the house is filled with bright pink cosmos grown from seed. I need to clear it soon, in time for the spring bulbs to go in.

There is plenty of new-ness going on also. The amazing golden yellow of the *Rudbeckia* makes me wish I had planted more, and the *Cobaea scandens* (cup and saucer vine), which has scrambled all over my tripods and covered the fences, is bursting into flower and couldn't be more beautiful.

WHAT TO DO IN YOUR VIRGIN GARDEN THIS MONTH

BUYING BULBS   If you've ordered bulbs earlier in the year, you can sit back smugly for a little longer, but if not, then get thee to a garden centre and buy the ones that make you swoon before anyone else gets their grubby little mitts on them. You want to give yourself the biggest choice and the freshest, firmest bulbs. If you haven't even thought about them until now, have a quick look at my suggestions for must-have bulbs on page 120 and use that as a starting point. If you've already ordered bulbs and are waiting patiently for them, stay well away from that section of the garden centre.

CLEARING UP   This is a good time to get out there and have a bit of a tidy-up. Pull out weeds that you missed the last time you were concentrating on such things and chop off anything on your perennials that you find 'unsightly'. This differs hugely from person to person, so I can't be prescriptive, but as a guide I remove anything brown and crispy, unless it is unquestionably beautiful (like a poppy or *Nigella* seedhead).

CUTTING BACK   This is entirely a common-sense exercise. If you look closely at your perennials, you will see that many of them will be at the end of their flowering time. These flowering stalks can now be removed at their base if they are thrown up from a rosette of leaves at ground level, or, if they flower on stalks which have leaves all the way up them, then cut these stalks to just above a pair of leaves, at a point that feels comfortable (for me, that's about one-half to two-thirds of the way down the plant). The aim is to get the plant to concentrate its growth back to its roots and have it looking nice and compact so it's not sprawling all over the place, but not to cut it back so much that you shock it to death. Remember, it has to photosynthesise through its leaves in order to feed itself. If you gave your plants the Chelsea Chop (see page 94) back in May, then they're probably still beautiful right now and you should just let them get on with being lovely. If not, then a general chop now will often give you another flush of flowers in a couple of weeks' time.

PRUNING SHRUBS   For shrubs, I use the same gut feeling for dealing with them as I do for perennials. Removing anything that looks hideous will generally be a good thing, and you can lightly prune shrubs to keep their shape. There is enough warm weather left for them to get over the shock of a light chop before the cold weather sets in. Minus the spent flowers and the flopping stems, your garden will suddenly have a new lease of life.

PLANNING YOUR BULB-PLANTING Take a good look at your flowerbeds and decide where you're going to plant your bulbs. Remember that the removal of any bedding plants or annuals will provide some space, but if you think you need more room than this, be ruthless and take out a few perennials and give them to friends or plant them elsewhere. I promise it'll be worth it. At the same time, if plants are too close together, now is a good time to space them out a bit better (and that often means removing a few extras).

TRIMMING HEDGES If you have a garden or live in an urban area, the chances are you have an established hedge somewhere in the vicinity. Now is the time to give it a trim in order to keep its shape. Evergreen hedges like privet, holly, yew, box, laurel, cedar and cypress can all be clipped into shape now, as any new growth will have enough time to ripen before it gets too cold. Deciduous hedges like beech and hornbeam are also best chopped now. Use your common sense when you're cutting: hedges with small leaves can be attacked with shears or clippers; larger-leaved hedges need their shoots individually cut with secateurs. As always, identify your hedge first before you go at it with choppers and loppers.

Mizuna while you wait

Mizuna is one of the prettiest of all the oriental leaves. It has a punchy flavour that renders it perfect for using in small quantities to sex up dull salads. Oriental leaves need a cooler growing environment if they are to become luscious and beautiful. If they get too hot, they will produce seed too rapidly (a process known as 'bolting').

The method of growing I like to use here is known as 'cut-and-come-again'. This simply means that you will be harvesting your produce when it is small, succulent and salad-ready (as opposed to stir-fry appropriate). By the middle of August, I'm a bit bored of doing nothing in the garden and have usually been unable to resist a trip to the local nursery which, at this time of year, is full of bulbs that I like to plant now in pots. They won't appear, though, until next spring, so the mizuna will ease the pain of looking at an otherwise empty pot. Of course, it goes without saying that doubling up with bulbs is not in the least bit essential for the production of lovely mizuna leaves, so leave them out and use a shallower vessel if you like.

YOU WILL NEED
A packet of mizuna seeds
Some bulbs you love I used tulips and muscari here (and see my project on page 182 for the ultimate layered pot of bulbs).
A large, wide pot 30cm diameter or more, and deep enough to plant bulbs in (if you wish). Tulips, for example, should generally be planted at around 15cm deep, so the pot needs to be at least 30cm deep to accommodate roots and watering room at the top.
Multi-purpose compost
A small amount of horticultural grit, or sharp sand

METHOD
First of all, plant your bulbs. Refer to the packet and fill your pot with compost to the depth of planting, sprinkling a layer (5mm or so is fine; it doesn't have to be exact) of grit or sharp sand at this level. This gives the bulbs an extra bit of drainage and prevents them from rotting in cold, wet soil. I have to be honest here, and say that I often don't bother with this and I haven't noticed any difference, but I do see the logic of it and always use grit if I have it to hand.

Now place your bulbs, pointy side up, on the compost. I put in as many as I can fit on the layer without them touching each other. Next, pour in more compost, firming down gently so that the pot is filled, but leaving a gap of 3–4cm between the top of the compost and the rim of the pot.

Clean and dry your hands, open the seed packet and pour the contents into your palm. Take small pinches of seeds and sow them thinly over the surface of your compost. You can't be accurate about this, and it really doesn't matter, because this is cut-and-come-again. Sprinkle the merest suggestion of some more compost very gently over the top of your seeds and firm down with a reassuring pat from your palm. Now water the whole thing, using a watering can with a fine rose, until you can see water coming out of the bottom of the pot. Cover with a wicker cloche or something similar if your pots are a target for squirrels or other creatures.

Put the pot in a sheltered spot – light shade is best – and make sure it stays moist. In just five or six days, leaves will appear, and they will be ready for cutting whenever you choose (but I think it's best to wait until they're about 10cm tall). You can harvest the whole lot in one go, or do it in bits, but be sure that you cut them a centimetre above the surface of the compost so they can re-sprout. Keep watering the pot, of course, and let it sit there outside all winter, by which time you will have forgotten about the bulbs. Suddenly, in springtime next year, little green tips will appear and your bulbs will delight you well into early summer.

Spinach for baby leaves

This is a lovely crop to start off in midsummer when you're not up for anything too taxing but need to get busy with something. Spinach is a vegetable that really does benefit from being grown at home; washing salad is excruciatingly dull, and with a bit of care, you needn't even think about washing this.

There are lots of plants known as 'spinach' – the two most common are true spinach (*Spinacia oleracea*) and leaf beet (*Beta vulgaris* subsp. *cicla*), which are basically beetroots grown for their leaves and include the beautiful Swiss chard. Here we use the ordinary 'true spinach', adopting a 'grab-them-while-they're-young' approach (always the best way to go with leaves as it gives no time for invertebrates to slime over and chow down on your crop, and means you get the tastiest bit). I grow my spinach in an old wine box or wide, shallow pots, so it's less vulnerable to slugs and because I think it looks pretty, but you can of course grow spinach in the ground, where you will get far more of it.

YOU WILL NEED

Spinach seeds

A container of your choosing

Compost I use ordinary multi-purpose compost with a bit of John Innes No. 2 added in for moisture retention. Spinach likes really fertile, moist soil, so if you want to grow it in the ground, then make sure this is what you provide. As long as this plant has moisture, it can cope with a little shade.

METHOD

This is a cut-and-come-again crop, so you don't have to worry too much about spacing and thinning. All you need to do is fill your pot or box with your compost mixture, and water it well before you sow any seeds. You can either sow the seeds in 'drills' (straight lines), which makes it slightly easier to get at the leaves, or just scatter them as evenly as possible over the surface of the compost. For drills, make a little ditch by drawing your finger or a pencil through the compost and sow the seeds thinly (by which I mean make sure as much as possible that they don't all land in one spot together). Repeat this process with each drill roughly 10cm apart.

Cover the seeds with compost, so they are about a centimetre beneath the surface, and pat it down gently. If you have watered well, then this surface sprinkling of compost will take up water of its own accord and you shouldn't have to water it.

Now all you need to do is put the container in a sheltered spot – lightly shaded is fine – and wait, making obsessively sure that the container doesn't dry out. You can

start harvesting at any time, but one day you'll find that the leaves are perfect, and you won't know how you know ... you'll just know. Pick each leaf at the base of that succulent green oval, and keep the container watered. The crop should soon re-sprout.

If you get the spinach bug (and it's hard not to, with such an obliging plant), then make sure you have a continuous supply by sowing another pot every three weeks, and moving the whole caboodle on to the kitchen window-sill when it gets to proper autumn (say, mid-October).

TO EAT I like to eat baby spinach raw for its creaminess. It seems rather a shame to cook something so perfect. My only concession to this is to let it wilt a tiny-weeny bit under the heat of some bacon bits and a cut-up, sunset-yolked boiled egg.

A bay window

I happen to like a little frippery in the garden. Small bits of topiary like cute box lollipops fill me with delight (witness the Valentine's ivy heart on page 254). I realise, though, that this isn't everyone's cup of tea. Here's a piece of quick topiary that does more than just make me giggle. This circle of bay is a really useful device for framing something in the garden, either near to it, or far away. What I'm trying to say is that it's a ready-made, easily moved view-maker. Bay looks fabulously smart and orderly (a good thing in my garden); it is also an indispensable kitchen herb. Left to its own devices, bay can become a very large tree, but because it tolerates being clipped so well, it can live very happily in a relatively small container for years.

YOU WILL NEED
1 bay plant (*Laurus nobilis*) Pick one that hasn't been topiarised and is nice and bushy. At this time of year you can always find this sort of thing left sad and neglected at the back of the shelves in the local nursery.
Some heavy-gauge wire Either galvanised, copper or plastic-coated to make the frame.
Wire cutters
Pliers
A beautiful terracotta pot Remember, this is a long-term pot.
A few crocks for drainage
John Innes No. 3 compost
Some green wire ties or inconspicuous green garden twine

METHOD
First make the frame by deciding how large you want it, and what shape. A circle is the simple route. It's best to make the frame out of two identically-sized circles of wire, held together at approximately 4cm apart with more stiff wire. This will make the frame sturdy and less likely to fall flat. You also need to leave some wire at the bottom of each circle to create a 'stake' so you can plunge it into the pot.

When you're happy with your frame, fill your pot with a few crocks, then the compost, and plunge the frame into it. Make sure it is sturdy enough, although it doesn't matter if it is a little wobbly because the plant will eventually help to anchor it.

Now plant your bay directly in the middle and in front of the frame, and separate the foliage in the centre, picking two or three of the longest shoots on either side and attaching them to the frame carefully with green wire ties or twine. Snip the remaining shoots off the plant and water the whole thing in well. Bay is happy in a sheltered spot (no freezing wind, please) and can cope with light shade if it needs to.

All that remains to do is to keep tying in the shoots until you have built up a really beautiful shape. When the two sides eventually meet at the top of the circle you may decide to keep going round again and achieve a thicker look, or just tie the last bit in and start snipping to maintain the shape.

For maintenance, apart from keeping it well-watered, you can give it a liquid seaweed feed each spring to compensate for the nutrients it lacks by being in a pot. In year two, you could also give it a boost by removing the top layer of compost (say 4–5cm) and replacing it with new.

Natural mists for sunny days

This is a lovely idea for a summer party in the garden or a trip to the beach. When it gets hot they are a real luxury, and a great present, I find, for pregnant ladies, or anyone who gets over-heated. Here I use lavender, mint and rosemary, but experiment with other combinations, like lemon verbena, cucumber – or anything edible.

YOU WILL NEED **Plastic misting bottles** Available, often in travel sizes, from all good pharmacies.
Water
Sprigs of lavender, mint and rosemary
A hot day

METHOD Simply fill your misting bottle with water and put a sprig of your chosen herb into each bottle. Any fragrant, edible plant will work – these are just suggestions. Label it prettily and pass around on a hot summer's day. That's it.

Autumn

September

It's that time of year, when everyone goes back to school, people become suddenly obsessed with writing lists of things to do, and *Vogue* is as thick as your doorstep. It rains and it rains until you think it'll never stop, and then the next minute you get drenched in warm sunshine. It's lucky that the bustling busybody in me decides to make an appearance, because at this time the garden is really crying out not only for some TLC but also for a sterner, more rational hand than the summer allows.

All my summer bedding came out in one fell swoop – a lovely job and uniquely satisfying; my *Nicotiana* was utterly gorgeous and just the thing when it was in its prime, but it has done the job of filling the gaps as my more permanent and treasured perennials and shrubs have been filling out. My aim is to have no need for summer bedding next year, apart from the odd must-have addition here and there. With these flowers gone, and all the errant weeds removed, it feels like the garden can breathe again.

The biggest change is the removal of my temporary sweet pea screen (see page 34), which was still giving me loads of flowers but its leaves had fallen victim to mildew. I am rather loving not having the distraction of those sweet peas, and after an initial wobble about planting a proper hedge in its place, I am now resolved to do just that next month (for October is the time for planting such things).

I've been lurking in the garden centre again, amassing various autumn and winter plants for the pots on the terrace, but by far the most dramatic bit of work I've done is to make sure there is enough space for my bulbs. This has meant doing some lifting and moving of various perennials (the shrubs stay right where they are, thank you) and rather too much time standing in the middle of the lawn with a calculator deciding which bulbs, and how many of them, to put where. The first to go in were a load of alliums, along with lots of irises and daffodils under the trees in The Apple Garden. When it came to planting the last allium I was scandalised to find that I had under-ordered and quickly had to get on the phone and ask for more. This last batch will go in next month. The tulips will wait until November, to avoid them getting a disease called tulip fire.

WHAT TO DO IN YOUR VIRGIN GARDEN THIS MONTH

PLANTING BULBS

It's time to tidy up and make way for some bulbs, so rip out your summer bedding and pull out any weeds that have crept through the net. The sooner you get your bulbs in (excluding tulips, that is) the better. If you're planning on planting a lot of them, then it's a good idea to invest in a bulb planter, which makes the whole process much easier. All you do is plunge it into the ground to the required depth (look on your packet of bulbs for this information, but as a general rule, bulbs should be planted at two to three times their height), and remove a cylinder of earth, put the bulb in the bottom and then release the clod over the top – easy as pie. The big trick with bulbs is not to be mean; make sure they're in groups of five or more. Keep the group numbers odd, because even numbers look wrong somehow. Try to cram as many bulbs in as possible without damaging the roots of neighbouring plants, and taking heed of the planting distances stated on your packet. Keep them in the middle or towards the back of your flowerbed, making sure there is something low-growing in front of your groups which can 'take over' visually when the bulbs have died down. It's also vitally important to mark where you have put your bulbs. Planting is hard work and you don't want it going to waste. If you don't mark the position of each bulb, or at least of each group of bulbs, then you will forget they are there and dig them up by mistake. I use cheap white plastic plant labels, pushed deep into the soil so that just their tips are showing and only I really notice that they are there.

One last word on bulbs: you can carry on planting well into November so don't worry if life is too busy right now – the important thing is that they get planted at some point. If you do need to store bulbs, put them in a cool, dry place. I put mine in an unheated room inside the house – not everyone has somewhere perfect like a larder or a garage that isn't damp, and it's damp you really do want to avoid.

LOVING YOUR LAWN

If you've got a lawn, then September is the perfect time to do some work on it while the weather is still warm-ish and it's a pleasure to be outside. Even though I'm the last person who would want a pristine lawn, I still want a lush one, and the best way of making that happen is to do the following.

First, mow your lawn, then get yourself a spring-tine rake and scarify it. This simply means quite roughly pulling the rake along the whole lawn and removing all the 'thatch' that has built up, such as moss and dead grass. You'll be amazed at how much there is. When you've finished going one way, change direction and go across, scarifying the whole lawn again but from a 90° angle, and there will be more of the stuff. Grass clippings and thatch can go on your compost heap if you

have one, but only in thin layers, along with other, different material. If you put too many grass clippings together in one place, they become a big, slimy mass. Once you've finished this, it might look a bit sad, but your lawn will thank you in the springtime for the extra light, air and moisture you have given it. If you have bare patches of lawn, then now is also the time to repair them by sowing some grass seed, or using a ready-grown roll of turf.

CHOPPING YOUR LAVENDER If you've got new lavender and trimmed it of its flowers a few weeks ago (see page 142), now is the time to cut it back hard. This will feel utterly wrong and brutal but it really is the best way to get lovely, hummocky, bushy lavender for next year. If you look into the centre of the plant you'll see little leaves sprouting from what looks like old, brittle wood. This should give you the confidence to go in and chop it to about half its original size, keeping the outside shoots shorter than those in the centre to create a gorgeous mound. If your lavender is inherited and bigger, then go a little more carefully, making sure there are lots of little bits of new growth below your intended cut. Be brave, though, because leggy lavender is really not worth having, and it would be better to experiment and risk losing a plant than soldier on with something that looks hideous. Lavender grows quickly and really rewards you if you treat it properly right from the start, so if your inherited monstrosity keels over, then just rip it out and replace it with a new one.

FIRING UP YOUR WINDOW-BOX If you made a summer window-box then now is a good time to give it an autumn facelift (see page 137).

BEING TIDY The main message for autumn in the garden is husbandry: if you keep things relatively tidy, picking up fallen leaves from lawns and paths and removing most dead material from your flowerbeds, then you'll prevent diseases getting to your treasured shrubs and, by doing so, keep the garden looking beautiful for winter.

Mint for winter cocktails

The gratifying thing about mint is the way in which it spreads itself about. Some people regard it as a nuisance, but you'll never have a problem with mint if you grow it in containers. If you want it in the garden, just plant some in a large plastic pot and bury the pot in the ground. I like to take advantage of mint's brilliant ability to spread, for proper mint sauce and that taste of summer in our Christmas drinks.

Mint spreads by using 'runners', which are basically roots with little baby plants on them. It usually dies down over the winter, like any sensible perennial, but you can pot up some of the roots and bring them indoors, tricking them into making an appearance when you need them most.

YOU WILL NEED

1 mint plant that you love Everyone has their favourite – I love the furry-leaved *Mentha suaveolens* (apple mint).
A clean, sharp knife Like a penknife or a craft knife.
A small pot (15cm diameter) with its own saucer I like to use small terracotta long-toms because they look pretty, and remember, this will be in your kitchen.
Some multi-purpose compost

METHOD

If your mint is in a pot, turn it upside down and take the whole lot out. You'll be able to see the roots clearly snaking around the sides of the pot. If you're using mint that is in the ground, just dig up a small amount of it, trying not to damage the roots.

Once you've located one of the long, white roots with tiny green nodules on it, cut this off the plant and divide it into sections, each about 4cm long, favouring those with lots of nodules. Re-plant the original in its old spot or pot outside and get ready to plant your cuttings.

Fill your pot with compost almost to the top and simply lay four or five of your sections on to the surface and cover them with a layer of compost – 2cm should do it. Water the whole thing well and bring it indoors by a window. In just a few days you'll see little green leaves appearing, which is just magical. It will continue growing through the winter months and on into spring, when you can put it outside again.

MORE

The ultimate mint cocktail is a Mojito. Just bash a few mint leaves with two tablespoons of sugar and a splash of soda water, until the sugar has dissolved and you can smell the mint. Add the juice of a lime and a measure of light rum, shake with ice and strain into a glass full of crushed ice and more mint leaves, topping up with more soda water.

Hyacinths for waxy-scented winter days

I have always had a love-hate relationship with hyacinths. Sometimes I'm head-over-heels about them, and other times I find their scent gives me a headache. But the love usually wins out in the end, particularly given that prepared hyacinths can be up and blooming slap bang in the middle of winter. I plant them in baskets to soften their rather military look, but you can use any container, so long as it has the usual drainage holes in the bottom. If you want to display them in a pretty china bowl, then plant them in plastic pots and add moss to cover the un-pretty bits when you come to bring them in.

Hyacinthus are bulbous perennials that come from rocky slopes high up in western and central Asia. Left to their own devices, they are spring-flowering but you can buy 'prepared' hyacinths that have been kept in cold storage and tricked into flowering much earlier. This is indoor-gardening at its loveliest.

YOU WILL NEED

Hyacinth bulbs My favourites right now are 'Jan Bos' which is a fantastic shade of pink, and the waxy white 'Carnegie'.
A plastic-lined basket Mine is 35cm in diameter.
Multi-purpose compost or special compost called 'bulb fibre' This is available at most good garden centres. Bulb fibre is specially formulated for indoor bulb-planting, containing ingredients that keep the compost fresh over long periods. Multi-purpose compost is fine, but bulb fibre is better if you can get it.

METHOD

Make sure your basket is lined with plastic, and that the plastic has some holes in it to let water drain out. You can usually buy baskets that are already lined from florists, but it's easy to line your own by sewing a plastic bag into it, using a big needle and some cotton thread. As mentioned above, people can and do use beautiful china bowls for their hyacinths, but watering just the right amount is tricky and turns me into a bag of nerves, so a basket, placed on a tray to save my furniture, is my compromise.

Fill the basket with compost and plonk in your bulbs so that their tips are at the same level as the rim of the basket. You want them close together, but not touching. Now cover them with more compost, so that the tips of the bulbs are peeping out of their brown bed.

Water the basket so that the compost is dampened but not sodden and put the whole thing in a cool, dark place. This could be a shed or a garage, or even a downstairs loo or spare room – just make sure there's no heating on. I keep mine (covered with a large pot-saucer) in my basement. It's important to keep things dark

at this stage because you want the bulbs to think they're underground and it's spring-time. This will trick them into growing roots and shoots.

Keep the poor things in their cold, dark prison for three or four months, watering lightly every now and then to make sure they don't dry out. When they get to about 7cm high you can bring them out into the relative light and warmth of your kitchen or living room and they will start to flower. You can cover the surface of the compost in between the plants with moss if you don't like the look of the bare earth, and add twigs if you like, both to support the blooms (which can sometimes get rather top-heavy) and to add a touch of quirkiness to the arrangement.

To prolong the display, put them back into the cool at night-time, but this is always a bit of a faff so I just let them go for it.

A cascade of *Viola*

This is an age-old way of displaying plants that I love because you can have three pots of something but take up the space of only one. You absolutely don't have to use *Viola* – any small plant that will cover the sides of a pot will do – it's just that violas are so cheerful with their smiley faces that I can't help buying lots of them whenever they come on sale in autumn.

YOU WILL NEED

Viola The individual ones sold in polystyrene cells lend themselves to this project because it's easy to squish each individual plant around the sides of the pots. But if you can only find large pots, don't worry, because they are very easy to divide and great value for money. For my bottom pot, of 33cm diameter (see below), I used 5 plants around the edge. You could also use pansies, which are just bigger, frillier versions of the *Viola*.

3 pots of different sizes Mine are 11cm, 21cm and 33cm diameter, but that isn't set in stone. The aim is simply to have enough room around the sides of each pot to plant your violas in once the next pot is plonked in the centre of it.

Multi-purpose compost

METHOD

If you've bought plants in large pots, divide them into smaller ones by gently prising the roots apart. You want to end up with a number of small plants, but in good enough clumps to fill out quickly.

Fill each of your pots with compost and arrange them in a tower, slightly burying the two smaller pots within the compost on which they sit in order to give them a solid foundation. Now take each plant and squish it into the space left around the sides of first two pots, spacing them about 10cm apart. Make sure they are firmly planted and at the same depth they were in their plastic pots or polystyrene. Also, it's good practice to leave a small space between the top of the compost and the rim of the pot as this will make watering a whole lot easier. Finally, put a single plant (or more if you can fit them in) in the last small pot.

Water the whole tower very carefully, making sure that all the compost has been dampened and there is water coming out of the bottom of the biggest pot. This will take a while, but important things do take time. Keep watering periodically, making sure that the compost never dries out, and in a few weeks' time the flowers will have completely covered the sides of the pots.

The ultimate layered pot of bulbs

Bulb-planting, along with tidying up, makes up 90 per cent of the work to do in a garden when autumn comes along, and bulbs are some of the most delectable plants around. But even if you don't have a garden, there's no reason why you shouldn't have the pleasure of all things bulbous. In fact, most bulbs are totally fine in pots, and if anything, the planting is easier and far less time-consuming with this method. For this pot, I've chosen bulbs that will start flowering in January and last all the way through until June – that's six months of gorgeousness – so although it'll just look like a pot with earth in it over the winter, all will be forgiven and forgotten as soon as the first shoots come up in early spring. One last thing: it's best to do two or three or even four of these – you'll be so glad you made the effort.

YOU WILL NEED

Bulbs Here is my list, but if you go online, or to a nursery that has a great selection, you'll be able to chop and change with abandon. The only thing you really have to pay attention to is the time of flowering in order to get a succession of blooms.
In my pot I have:
Crocus tommasinianus 'Barr's Purple': flowers December and January
Iris reticulata 'Cantab': flowers February and March
Narcissus 'Pipit' (a small daffodil): flowers April
Tulipa 'Spring Green': flowers May
Allium neapolitanum 'Grandiflorum' (with relaxed, star-like blooms): flowers June
Large pots Mine are 33cm diameter and 33cm deep. The wider the pot, the more bulbs you can cram in – they need to be close together but not touching.
Multi-purpose compost and a handful of added sand or grit This is to keep it from getting soggy.
Some kind of pot-protection This is very important because squirrels and birds love to dig for carefully planted bulbs. I use bamboo cloches, which I cram tightly over the sides of the pot.

METHOD

Sort out your bulbs, not in order of date, but in size. The biggest ones, no matter what their flowering date is, should go at the bottom, and the smallest ones should be planted last. Because there are many layers here, the bottom lot of bulbs will probably be much deeper than they ideally prefer. Don't worry, they'll make it up anyway, but nevertheless, I put them as high up as possible, whilst still leaving room for the rest of the bulbs. So fill your pot about one-third full with compost and start layering.

You need to place each bulb as near as possible to its neighbour without it actually touching. I always start by making a circle around the outer edge and work towards the middle. When you've finished one layer, cover the bulbs with a layer of compost so that you can't see them any more and there is a nice cushioned base for the next layer. Then start with the next largest bulb and continue until all your bulbs are in. The last bulbs should be planted underneath a layer of compost two to three times their size. Pat the whole thing down reassuringly and water it really well until you can see the water draining out of the hole at the bottom of the pot. Cover the pot with its cloche, leave the pot outside, and resolve to be patient. You will not be disappointed.

October

It's been a month both of change and no change. In the no-change category, I've been experiencing a third flush of flowering from both geraniums and *Lychnis*, along with more roses. But in other ways, there's been a seismic shift in the garden. I planted my long-awaited hedge in yew, using baby 60cm-high plants with the knowledge that the best things come to those who wait. Of course, I could have bought an instant hedge but where's the fun(ds)? I have big plans for this hedge: the dream is to grow it higher than most tall people and cut shapes in it at eye-height – portholes, or hearts even – for tantalising glimpses of the garden behind it. It's a bold move, because I'm hiding a large part of the garden, but my philosophy, as always, is that if it doesn't work, then I can remove it and try something else.

Long-term, this hedge will, I hope, satisfy my yearning for restful structure – something plain and green and solid, but I've given myself some instant structure in the form of new box shapes and some bay standards (a horticultural term for a plant that's been grown and clipped to look like a lollipop). It's amazing how much these have added to the look of the garden and I am feeling utterly smug and satisfied about having put them in.

We had a sharp frost this month which completely obliterated any remaining annuals in one fell swoop and goaded me into another much-needed tidy-up. I am not a neat-freak, but the process of tidying up is a seriously satisfying one. Not only does it keep the place looking good, but it also removes the distracting elements that prevent me from knowing what needs to be done. Once I banished the fripperies and the dead leaves, I was able to see what was needed for the long-term. I love gardening but I don't want to spend all my time doing it, so from now on, after my first blooming, blazing, bodacious, flowery summer, the emphasis will remain firmly with nurturing the shrubs and perennials that are already there – it is these plants that will eventually provide everything I need in terms of excitement in the spring and summer months.

WHAT TO DO IN YOUR VIRGIN GARDEN THIS MONTH

PLANTING
EVERGREENS

It's time to screw on your rational head and ask yourself some questions. When winter finally hits, the last perennial has gone underground and the leaves have dropped from your deciduous shrubs, what will you be left with? This is the perfect time to plant hardy evergreens if you feel the need for structure. There are very few gardens that are not improved by the addition of a couple of box balls, or yew columns, or holly standards. And you don't necessarily need bags of space to add structural elements – you can (and should) use standards or columnar shapes too. These take up very little ground space and cast hardly any shade. The plants I've suggested below also work equally well in their natural, bushy, spreading state, so they'll be perfect if you have large areas to cover and you want something low-maintenance. Remember that it's better to plant something than nothing – you can always take it out again if you hate it, but the chances are you'll be pleased as punch with whatever you've planted when it's winter and the garden looks smart and happy. Here are my favourite evergreens for formal, calming structure and hedging:

Buxus (box) is gorgeous. It can also be heart-breaking because sometimes it succumbs to disease, which, as it is slow-growing, can be tough. I think its beauty makes it more than worth the possible heartache. I use balls and cones dotted around, but box standards would, of course, be the ultimate extravagance. See page 194 for how to grow your own box balls. For hedging, box is most commonly kept low, to edge borders.

Ilex (holly) is a fabulous evergreen and can be clipped into all manner of shapes. It makes a brilliant hedge and is obviously a good burglar deterrent too. It's very useful to have some holly when Christmas comes round as well. It's worth knowing that you can get little holly standards, and that it comes in variegated (bi-coloured) forms. If you want a holly hedge, and you want berries, you have to make sure you get the right amount of male and female plants, so take advice from the nursery.

Taxus (yew) is, I think, utterly majestic as a hedge. I love the restful darkness of it and it is not as slow-growing as box. This is what I chose for my hedge, primarily because it can take glorious and fantastical amounts of clipping and shaping.

Laurus nobilis (bay) is slightly less hardy than my first three choices, but still essential in my garden as a structural evergreen. Obviously, it has the added benefit of being a delicious herb too, but I love it also because a bay standard is about a

quarter the price of a box one, and just as beautiful in its own way. Bay makes a great hedge too, although it wouldn't be my first choice if I lived up north.

PLANTING A HEDGE If you want to plant a hedge, this is the perfect time to do it. Make sure your ground is prepared as you would make a bed for the most precious of friends. Dig a trench at least a spade's depth, adding manure if you can get hold of it, or soil-improver which is sold in bags at most garden centres. If you ordered bare-root hedging plants earlier in the year, make sure you soak the roots for an hour or so before planting and take care to plant at the right depth (you'll see the soil mark on the plant). Hardy evergreens are tough, but they will still thank you for a fabulous start in life, so plant them carefully and firmly, making sure that the planting level is a few centimetres lower than the ground surrounding the trench, so that when you water, the water is contained and goes where you want it. Water them in properly by giving the ground a really good soak after planting. You want to encourage the roots to grow down, so if you water only a little (and this applies to all plants), the roots will run just below the surface and not down to reach the water table. Keep watering every day for a couple of weeks or more, letting your instinct guide you (for example, I would not water on a day that was freezing cold, but would rush out and give a good soak once the sun came out).

MULCHING This is only a suggestion, but if you have the time and can afford some bags of compost, it is well worth doing. Apart from making everything look gorgeously tidy, it will add a layer of warmth for the roots of your plants. Having said that, this is not essential, as you will be doing a proper mulching in springtime, when all your plants are ready to burst into life.

WASHING-UP This is the perfect time to get all your empty pots and seed trays sparkling so they are ready to use at a moment's notice. Use a bucket of soapy water, with a splash of thin bleach in it, and an old sponge to give everything a good clean.

PLANTING BULBS FOR A SPRING FLING In the spirit of rational forward-thinking, keep planting those bulbs, both in the ground and in pots for lots of spring and summer glamour (see page 182 for The ultimate layered pot of bulbs).

Microgreens

When autumn has lost its novelty, and all I'm noticing about my life is that it's both dark when I wake and getting dark at teatime, I start to yearn for newness and freshness. That's why I grow greens indoors at this time of year. If you've ever been to a fancy restaurant, or watched extremely accomplished chefs on telly, then you'll have come across these chic, little baby leaves. They are like the mustard and cress we used to grow at primary school, but taken to new heights. Microgreens are simply baby plants that you harvest when they're a few centimetres tall, instead of thinning them out and letting them grow on to reach their full potential. The baby seedlings often have the flavour of the eventual plant, but concentrated, which means that you only need a few of these scattered over a salad or a hunk of meat or fish to feel their full force. The best way to start is to find a packet of mixed microgreen seeds at the garden centre, but if you're a purist, then by all means choose one (or many) of the following, all of which make outstanding microgreens: mizuna (see page 156); radish; fennel; amaranth; any of the colourful, oriental mustards; rocket; cabbage; celery; and basil.

YOU WILL NEED

Packets of microgreen seeds (Or see above for suggestions.)
A container I use a plastic seed tray, 24cm x 38cm, but any container with holes at the bottom will do as long as it has a large surface area and fits inside a bright window-sill.
Multi-purpose compost
A tray One slightly larger than your container, into which you can water.

METHOD

It couldn't be easier. Just fill your seed tray with compost, then pick the whole thing up and drop it on to your work surface a couple of times to settle the contents and remove any large air pockets (roots can't live on thin air, you know). Add some more compost if you need to, filling it almost to the top to maximise light for your seedlings. Don't worry about leaving a space between the surface of the compost and the top of the container, because you'll be watering from the bottom. Now sprinkle your seeds all over the surface of the compost, trying not to leave any big gaps. Don't be worried about sowing too thinly because your seedlings are never going to reach the stage where that sort of thing matters. As a guide, I sow an entire packet of approximately 750 seeds into my seed tray. All you need to do now is sprinkle some more compost over the top, just a tiny bit, so that the seeds are covered very finely. Some people like to use a sieve for this, but I just pick up a handful of compost and rub my palms together (gleefully) above the tray.

Now water your seeds by filling the tray underneath with water and letting the compost suck up the moisture. This avoids displacing your seeds. You'll know there's enough water when the compost feels damp to the touch, at which point, if there's still a lot of water in the tray, you should pour it away.

Leave the tray on its window-sill and let the warmth of your house help the seeds to germinate. This will take two days or so, depending on the type of seed, and within two to three weeks, your microgreens will be ready to harvest. Sprinkle them on everything you can think of for that punchy freshness in the winter months. A small bowl filled with mixed microgreens and dressed with truly awesome vinaigrette is perhaps one of the most luxurious things you can give yourself at this time of year.

MORE   As soon as I start harvesting, I begin again with another seed tray, in order to keep up supplies. And, of course, you can and should grow microgreens in spring and summer too (when they will grow more quickly, and outside).

Slow topiary, for beauty and bones

I learned very quickly that it is the structural, evergreen plants that are the 'must-have' plants in any garden. These are the 'key pieces' around which all your other plants revolve. As long as you have them, your outside space will be beautiful and serene all year round. A gorgeous evergreen shrub is a wonderful thing, and perfect if you have the space, but if you topiarise box, then you not only have the evergreen, but you also have it contained, and, as if that weren't enough, you can clip it into weird and wonderful shapes. Of course you can buy box topiary everywhere, but because it takes time and attention to achieve these shapes, they are expensive, and often the quality is poor. To make your own is not only deeply satisfying, but it also requires the kind of 'wax on, wax off' commitment that makes you a better person somehow.

Buxus sempervirens (box) is the plant of choice here, because it is slow-growing, evergreen and small-leaved; all attributes that make it perfect for clipping. The best time to plant them is in the autumn, so that they can put on root growth before next year when you will start clipping. Below is a quick guide on how to make a box ball from scratch, grown in a container. If you want to grow your box in the ground, just make sure the patch is dug over, with a handful or two of soil-improver or some well-rotted manure, and make a small 'wall' of earth around the plant once you've put it in the ground to stop the water from trickling away when you douse it (see page 30 for planting a shrub).

YOU WILL NEED

Box plants My advice is to buy a six-pack of plants, often sold as box 'hedging' and widely available in most garden centres. These are plants that have been grown from cuttings and are very cheap. You can of course go for something larger (or even ball-like) but it rather defeats the purpose of doing it yourself and getting as much bang for your buck as possible.

Containers Make them terracotta, and 25–30cm in diameter, so that the plants have lots of room to grow and you won't have to re-pot for some time.

Pieces of broken pot or polystyrene To be placed over the hole at the bottom of each of your pots.

John Innes No. 2 compost

Granular fertiliser Mix this with your compost at the level stated on the packet.

And eventually, some clippers (See My essential tools on page 24.)

METHOD Water the plants thoroughly before you do anything. I usually put them in a tray of water for 30 minutes just to make sure the roots are saturated. Meanwhile, fill as many pots as you want balls with your John Innes No. 2 and fertiliser mix, not forgetting to put a crock over the hole at the bottom of each pot to prevent it getting blocked by heavy compost. My feeling on this is that if you've bought six plants, then plant all of them!

Plant your box with care and love in each pot, making sure their roots aren't going round in a circle (you may have to muss them up a little if the plants are a bit pot-bound). Make sure the compost is firmly pressed down but not compacted, and water the whole thing thoroughly from above, aiming the stream of water down the main stem from the top. I always water tough evergreens like this, believing (without a shred of research to back me up) that they will thank me for simulating a good rain shower.

Now you have to play the waiting game, but don't, whatever you do, leave your plants to languish in a corner. They may not look like very much right now but they are VIPs in the making, and you need to treat them as such. They are fully hardy but, even so, don't let them get thrashed about by wind and snow, or peed on by dogs or cats, or scratched around by squirrels. Do not let them dry out, or get too sodden. Be nice.

You will know when to start clipping – you'll have an idea in your head of how big your box ball is going to be. This idea will have much to do with the size of the pot; and suddenly you will hear them ask you to tidy them up. The best time to begin is in the late spring, after the plant has put on a little bit of new growth. This growth will be pale and gorgeous. You won't want to clip it, but you should. The first cut will probably be at the top, because plants like to grow UP. And shaving new growth off the top will encourage the plant to get bushy, and your ball will begin to take shape. Little and often is totally the key here. As a guide, confine your snipping to between the months of May and September. For really dense, tight shapes, clip twice, once in May or June, and again in August or September. Each time you snip, the plant will get bushier, and that's what you want: a lovely dense ball of box.

I'm not sure it's necessary to tell you how to clip box into a sphere, except to say that it is best done by eye, with sharp scissors or clippers, and that standing back and observing is as important as the actual doing of it. If you lack faith in yourself, then just stick a piece of masking tape around the plant to the desired girth, and one over the top, and snip between these markers. Remember always that less is more.

If you are growing your box in pots, they can be moved around for maximum impact. You can keep them at a certain size, or, if you like, pot them into larger containers and keep going.

Once you've got the hang of making balls, try a cone or a lollipop, or a square. And it's a good idea to keep your clippers clean by washing them in bleach to avoid passing on box blight or other nasties. It's also good practice to feed your box plants during the growing season (March to September) with a liquid seaweed feed.

Turn over for pictures

Christmas wrapping paper

It seems totally wrong to be thinking about Christmas in October, but I put this recipe here because we seem to have quite a few autumn birthdays in our family, so I find that making wrapping paper now sort of suits me. The other reason is that you can gather fallen leaves in abundance, before they get soggy and un-usable. At this time of year there's lots of leaf-collecting to be done anyway, to clear pathways (there's an enormous sycamore tree slap bang in front of our house and we have to sweep almost daily to get out of the front door) and for making leaf-mould (see page 206).

YOU WILL NEED

Lots of fallen leaves I like to use huge sycamore or oak leaves because they cover more area and have a beautiful shape, but literally anything will do, as long as it is fairly flat.
Some kind of large, flat surface to work on outside, or in a well-ventilated room, like a garage A trestle table would be the perfect thing but I use a piece of plywood on the ground.
A roll of paper I use plain red, but brown parcel paper from the post office would work beautifully and wallpaper lining is good too.
Glue stick
Coloured spray I love gold or silver.

METHOD

If you can't use your leaves immediately, then keep them in a plastic bag so they don't go totally brittle. Choose a still, dry day to spray. Unroll the paper, lay the leaves down on it artfully and stick them to the paper with the merest smudge of glue stick. Now spray over the leaves, until the paper is completely covered. Go away for a bit and let the whole thing dry, then remove the leaves to reveal your paper. Keep going until you have enough wrapping paper, and then it's done.

MORE

I often spray the other sides of the leaves and stick them into bowls of fruit or use them to decorate the table. Small, sprayed (or unsprayed) leaves look great as tags on presents – as always, the possibilities are endless.

An autumn table

After the abundance of spring and summer blooms, autumn and winter are seasons when I often feel bereft of ideas when it comes to decorating a table. It's probably obvious, but I don't go in for bought cut-flowers much (unless I'm lucky enough to be sent a bunch of blooms), and whilst I'd give my eye teeth to have something different every week or fortnight, I know myself, and I know that just won't happen, so my objective with any table decoration is that it should last weeks, rather than days, and be changeable at the drop of a hat. The sizes and shapes I give here simply stem from the size of my table and tray, so reduce or expand as you see fit.

YOU WILL NEED

Bags of sphagnum moss This is available in good nurseries. It's always useful to have sphagnum moss hanging around, particularly in the run-up to Christmas. If you keep it damp in a plastic bag and don't let it dry out, it lasts for months.

Little pots of whatever you love Bright pink cyclamen, heather and thyme are my top buys at this time of year. The number of plants will depend on the size of your tray (see below).

Some ivy with small and gorgeous leaves If you can't find these sold in little pots, then buy a larger one and divide it up – easy.

Ivy candles stuck with rosehips Or you can use other berries (see page 230).

Fruit, gourds, nuts and other autumn things

A tray Whatever size and shape fits comfortably in the middle of your table.

Small terracotta pots of 11cm diameter These can be found in big garden centres very cheaply and it's worth buying quite a few because they always come in handy. I like this size because it will hold the 9cm plastic pots also sold in garden centres.

Multi-purpose compost

METHOD

I'm not going to tell you how to arrange pots of flowers, just make a few suggestions. If you need to divide your ivy up, then do so first. You only really need one long tendril of leaves per pot, and ivy can take just about any kind of treatment, so don't be worried about prising it apart in a few places. Re-plant each spray in its own pot using ordinary multi-purpose compost, water them well and place them evenly over your tray, remembering that the ivy leaves are going to hide some of the terracotta by falling suggestively over the rim of the tray on to the table. To this end, if your tray is circular, put these pots of ivy around the edge.

Next, simply plonk your flowers into the pots without bothering to remove them from their plastic. This means you can replace them easily with no mess when you are tired of them. Pansies are great for this too, but they're a bit more fiddly to work with indoors, as, in my experience, they suffer from being too warm. That doesn't mean you shouldn't have them, though, just alternate them with some cyclamen or heather so they get time outdoors every couple of days.

Once you have filled your tray with flowers, leaves and candles, get your moss and use it to cover anything un-pretty. Sit down at the table to do this and turn the tray around so you get an eater's view of your creation. If you like, you can also use the moss to hide the sides of the tray. Water any plant that is dry, and place fruit and nuts and whatever else you like around the outside to complete the display. If you're using heather or cyclamen, they'll be happy inside for a good few weeks. You'll need to deadhead cyclamen to keep them flowering, and with heather, you can just let it dry out slowly in its pot. Obviously, try to keep temperatures cool, at least overnight.

MORE You can use this template again for some late-winter loveliness: just replace the cyclamen with some early-spring bulbs – here (see overleaf) I've used *Iris danfordiae* – and the pansies with some tiny pots of skimmia, both of which can be planted out in the garden when they're no longer required at the table.

Turn over for pictures

November

Despite the vilification that November gets for its grey chilliness, I often find myself sighing with relief when it finally comes. The truth is that, if you've been even remotely good, you will probably have done most of your autumn work by now, and the slowing down of growth means that most jobs can wait a week, or even a month or more before you get round to them. This month, I did practically nothing outside, except the gentle raking of some leaves and the brushing off of heavy snow from my evergreens. The cold kept me 'hostage' inside, tending to my hyacinths, paperwhites (forced narcissi) and microgreens (see page 192) – and eating a respectable amount of cake, of course.

I don't remove leaves that land in my flowerbeds – it's a thankless job and I would only be removing natural goodness, so I leave well alone. The exception to this is that I do have a huge sycamore tree in one corner of the garden which dumps vast amounts of leaves on one particular border – these I remove because there are just so many of them. The argument for clearing leaves off flowerbeds is that they harbour pests and diseases. It's an argument I am studiously ignoring because I want a low-maintenance garden. If I end up with borders that are riddled with disease, I will let you know.

And then we have the issue of tidiness. The look of the garden right now is, well, it's a bit squiffy to say the least. I've put in some structural evergreens to pull it out of ramshackle and into respectable. For me, these additions have done enough to satisfy my particular standards, but I realise that this look may not be everyone's cup of tea. In this case, if you have chosen to do the 'romantic and wafty' thing in terms of planting, then you will have to be prepared to do a bit more work at this time of year if you want a super-smart winter garden. My guess is, though, that if you're of a tidier disposition, then you will anyway have opted for plants that give less waft and more structure, or you'll have stuck to a small range of plants which will give a more uniform, restful look in the colder months.

WHAT TO DO IN YOUR VIRGIN GARDEN THIS MONTH

TULIP-PLANTING   Your tulips can finally be planted: plant masses ... and then add some more.

MAKING LEAF-MOULD   Falling leaves on any lawn or path need dealing with this month, particularly if you have trees in your garden. The best way is to gather them up, stuff them in a black plastic bin bag, punch some holes in it, and leave it outside and out of sight for a year or two while it rots down into gorgeous, precious leaf-mould, which you can use to add to compost, or top-dress your pots with. I love making leaf-mould, mainly because it takes so little effort and gives such fabulous results, but also because the idea of leaving something behind the shed to rot should by rights be a source of hideous guilt – this, blissfully, is not. If you want things to rot down a little more quickly, then you can mow over the leaves with the lawnmower on a high setting to chop them up a bit before they go in their bags.

WARMING YOURSELF   It's November, and if you have lots of twiggy debris, then it's the perfect time for a fire. Obviously, make sure things are as dry as possible to avoid too much smoke, and check with the neighbours first, but I find that the smell of a bonfire on a cold day is positively welcoming. I use one of those metal fire bins that you can find in DIY stores, and I sit outside for a while with a hot drink, adding my twigs and diseased material, bit by bit, and doing some judicious prodding from time to time.

PROTECTING YOUR POTS   If you have tender plants in pots, then it's time either to bring them indoors or to cover them with horticultural fleece – a sort of cobwebby material that looks ghostly but will save them from ruin. It's also a good idea to wrap expensive terracotta pots up in bubble-wrap in case they crack when it's frosty. I'm an advocate of both of the above actions, but I very rarely actually carry them out, preferring instead to see if my plants and pots will survive – but then I live in the south, so it's your choice. What I tend to do is group pots together to keep each other warm, and I also make sure that they never get too much water and are raised up off the ground, where possible, with those little pot-feet.

MOVING PERENNIALS   If you need to move any of your hardy perennials, then now is a good time to do it; just try to do it on a day when the ground isn't rock-hard with frost, and if you're in doubt about it, then leave it until the spring. Likewise, you can also take root cuttings of hardy perennials now, so that you can have lots of free plants for next year. See page 208 for instructions on how to do this.

Root cuttings for clouds of anemone

When you're filling a new garden, plants are expensive. I'm all for instant gratification, but there are some plants that are easy to propagate and that will eventually spread anyway. If you spent money to achieve a full effect instantly, you'd be removing plants and having to give them away in a few years. I'm talking perennials here, and specifically *Anemone* x *hybrida* (Japanese anemone), which is one of the most welcome sights in any garden in late summer and autumn. It's also happy in the shade, making this the most useful and beautiful of garden plants. Of course you could get these as plug plants from a supplier – it just seems silly not to do it yourself as they reproduce so easily, and also because you can do this in winter when there's less going on.

YOU WILL NEED **A Japanese anemone plant** One that you love and want lots of – they come in blushing pinks or purest white and all are gorgeous. If you have one growing in your garden, then use that, or go out and buy one, knowing that you'll get a return on your investment.
A clean, sharp knife I use a penknife rubbed with alcohol.
A clean plastic pot The size depends on how many cuttings you are taking; if it's lots and lots, then use a modulated seed tray, so that each cutting has its own little pot.
Cuttings compost I use a mix of three-quarters bought seed and cuttings compost, and one-quarter horticultural grit.

METHOD Remove the plant from its pot, or carefully dig it up from the ground and locate the thickest root you can find. Don't worry if the roots aren't very thick – the first time I did this the roots were so spindly I thought they'd never work, but they did.

Cut this root off the plant, lay it on a work surface, and use your knife to divide it into sections about 3cm long. Now fill your pot or tray with the compost mix and bang it on the table a couple of times to settle the contents. Lay your cuttings on top of the compost, leaving 4 or 5cm of space between them. Each of these will produce shoots, create their own root systems and become a new plant. Take more than you anticipate needing, because some won't make it (that's gardening). Now cover your cuttings with a little more compost mix, or just horticultural grit if you have it to hand. Press down gently but firmly, and water the whole thing very carefully with the fine rose of a watering can, making sure that nothing gets dislodged.

Put the pot inside you kitchen window-sill or somewhere warmish to stimulate the roots to sprout. Make sure it doesn't dry out and in a few weeks green leaves will appear as if by magic. At this point, I would move the pot somewhere cooler, but still indoors for a few weeks, and then put it outside in a cold frame. If you don't have a cold frame, then somewhere else that's frost-free, like a front porch, would work. It's not that this plant won't withstand frost, it's just that it's so small, and the compost in the pot might freeze, which would destroy the new root system.

Creating a new root system takes time, so leave the pot and forget about it for a few months, making sure it doesn't dry out, of course – until each cutting has put on three or four leaves. At this point, you can be fairly confident that they are ready to be potted on. To do this, separate each plant really carefully, so that you disturb the roots as little as possible, and re-plant each one in its own 9cm pot, using multi-purpose compost. When these toddlers have grown into healthy little plants, which, for me, is when I can see roots appearing through the holes at the bottom of the pot, then they're ready to put in the garden. They like a moist, shady site.

You will have a small flowering plant which can go in the ground the following year. Increasing your stock like this is a long game in our instant world, but somehow when you're gardening, things seems to happen in the blink of an eye, so do have a go ... you won't regret it.

Verdigris for those with shallow pockets

Here's an easy way to display plants (or anything else for that matter) that looks a million dollars but costs only a few pounds at an art store. Verdigris is the green patina that appears when copper is exposed to weather. The resulting colour is actually extremely vibrant but is tempered by the brown of the copper beneath. The project below simulates this look, and is really a paint-effect, nothing more, but I include it because outdoor containers rendered in this way are utterly beautiful and add a certain gravitas to a garden, especially a new one. I use them endlessly when I am too busy to plant things straight away and need to display something in its plastic for a while. You can of course drill holes in the bottom and use these for actual planters.

YOU WILL NEED **Stainless steel containers** You can usually buy these in threes – little bucket-shaped ones – from supermarkets or DIY stores. For larger ones, go for large pails in hardware stores.
Newspaper and an old plate or piece of board
Quick-drying white primer Available from DIY stores. Make sure the can states it is suitable for metal.
One medium-sized paintbrush Mine is 4cm wide.
Acrylic paint Brown and pale green.
One large stencil brush Looks like a shaving brush but with a blunt end.
Spray varnish Available from art shops.

METHOD Put out some newspaper and paint the outside of each of your tins with the primer. It doesn't have to be perfect, just roughly covering the metal. Leave them to dry and then paint over again with the brown acrylic paint. Again, leave this to dry and then squirt out a small amount of the green on to an old plate or piece of board, put a little of it on the stencil brush and bash it down a few times on to some newspaper to make sure that the colour is evenly distributed on the brush and not too thick. Now artfully stipple your tin, making some areas greener than others to achieve a mottled texture.

When this is all dry, take the tins outside and spray liberally with spray varnish. It's worth doing quite a few of these, because you can never have too many of them, and they are brilliant for giving away to friends (with a plant inside, of course).

MORE You can use this method with plastic pots too, although you'll need to rub the smooth surface with some wire wool to provide a key for the paint.

A cacti-scape

This is one of the easiest and most satisfying indoor plant projects you can do in the winter. You fuss over it for an hour or so whilst you're making it, and then simply gaze at it until March when you'll be required to do a little light watering. Cute little pots of cacti are sold in most good garden centres. I used to buy these periodically and display them randomly on tables with other tiny things, but that was before I had children and my whole life became about preventing both mortal injury and the loss or breakage of precious things; so as well as moving all my favourite breakable things on to high shelves, safe from small, chubby hands, I planted up all my cacti in desert gardens which I could put out of reach.

Cacti are part of a group of plants known as succulents which have adapted very cleverly to extremely dry conditions by reducing or completely getting rid of their leaves and storing water in their stem tissue to use when times are tough. Most of them have spines instead of leaves, which occur around a growing point, and which protect the plant from moisture-hungry birds and beasts, and also cleverly condense precious droplets of water. You can buy cacti all year round in garden centres and nurseries where they are sold in tiny little plastic pots. They often become quite top-heavy and keep falling over, so it's a good idea anyway to put them somewhere more stable.

YOU WILL NEED **A few tiny cacti** Five or seven is fine. (I just like odd numbers.)
Some old newspaper
A shallow terracotta bowl, with its own saucer Mine is 30cm diameter.
Crocks Pottery or polystyrene.
Cacti compost Available in small bags from most good garden centres, or you can make your own by mixing two parts multi-purpose compost with one part coarse sand and one part perlite. Whatever you do, make sure the compost is dry before you use it.
Some play sand Use the very fine sand available in bags for children's sandpits and/or some very small gravel or horticultural grit; again, make sure this is dry.
A knife, a fork and a spoon

METHOD This project takes time, not because it is difficult, but because you have to be slow and steady in order not to spike yourself on the plants. You can, if you wish, use gloves, but I find these unwieldy, so I just go very slowly and carefully.

First, remove all the plants from their tiny plastic pots. You can do this either by folding up some newspaper and wrapping it round the cactus, gently pulling the plant out and laying it on its side, or by gently kneading the sides of the pot to dislodge the soil and just tipping the plant out, again, on its side.

Now prepare your bowl by covering the hole at the bottom with a broken piece of pottery or some polystyrene, and fill the bowl with the cacti compost. Next, you need to plant your cacti, so decide where you want them to be (and don't space them evenly … this is a desert-scape). Make a little hole in the compost and carefully lower in a cactus, firming the compost in around the base. This will take a while because you'll not want to touch the plants.

Once all your cacti are in, then you are ready to top-dress the bowl with as much sand and gravel as you wish, using a knife, fork and spoon to smooth or add texture.

That's it. Place it where it will get a good amount of light, but it doesn't have to be warm; next to a window in an unheated room is ideal. Do not water it – these plants don't want anything from you until springtime, at which point you can give the pot a small amount of tepid water once a week, being careful not to get any water on the plants themselves, and increasing the amount slightly at each watering. As a guide, I give mine about two cupfuls of water to start with, but by June or July, the watering has increased to a point where I can see the run-off coming out of the pot.

In late April or May, as long as the weather is lovely, put the bowl outside to get some proper sunshine. If you're lucky, your cacti will flower for you, but don't expect this, just be pleased if it happens. Flowering is very much dependent on conditions, particularly those cool, dry winter months, and it's hard to get it just right. You will definitely notice growth though, and this (for me, anyway) is uniquely thrilling for plants which seem so inherently still and statuesque. You'll need to stop watering around October time (again, gradually decreasing the amount), bring the plants back inside and let the bowl dry out over winter again.

If you've top-dressed your pot with play sand, this will disappear into the compost when you water your cacti. If you hate the look of the soil surface, then add small gravel instead, or do as I do and leave it until the autumn and then put more sand on top.

Turn over for a picture

Winter

December

Let's keep this short and sweet. Yes, you are right, I have been inside eating mince pies, but there has also been a winter wonderland outside because we have had lots of snow. Any garden, in any condition, looks fabulous in the snow and it coaxed me out of the Christmas fug to admire my garden in its white cloak. It was only while I was out there that I realised how naughtily remiss I had been in November when it came to tidying up. In an ideal world, the perfect gardener would use October and November to 'put the garden to bed'. In addition to cutting down her herbaceous perennials, and pruning her roses, this gardener would clean her canes and stakes and tidy them away, and she would wash and sterilise her seed trays and pots ready for next year. The flowerbeds would look bare but beautifully, heave-a-sigh-of-relief tidy. In reality, I still have lots of tidying to do in the flowerbeds – there are seedheads and there is dead foliage that needs clearing and cutting away – but the weather and lack of time mean that this will have to wait (and I know from experience that the garden won't keel over and die just because I wasn't a good girl). I did, however, tidy up my pots and canes, quickly and without too much washing and wiping ... after all, there were snowball fights and hot chocolate to be had.

Much of my gardening life in December centres around Christmas. Nurturing hyacinths and *Hippeastrum* (see pages 174 and 232) is top of my list, and – now that I have a front door visible from the street – the whole wreath thing has taken on new significance. This year I was so short on time that I decided to try something different (no wiring required), which you can find on page 226.

This is traditionally the time for some good old 'armchair gardening'; it's a time for reflection. I know instinctively that the first winter in a new garden is not the moment to think about making changes to the layout; the garden needs another year or two to bed down and show me my mistakes. Likewise, at a time when I would usually be thinking about ordering new plants and seeds, I am stopping myself sternly. It's so easy to forget everything you put in once it has died down in the winter, and I have to remind myself constantly that there is not even an inch free for any more plants. As I've said before, I planned this as a low-maintenance garden, not one in which I plan and plant a 'fresh look' each year. All my plants are babies, and I need to give them time and space to grow.

WHAT TO DO IN YOUR VIRGIN GARDEN THIS MONTH

DOING THE DECEMBER TIDY If the weather is on your side, then do try to find an hour to tidy up a bit if you haven't already … it will make you feel good. But if it's all too much, don't worry – the tidying can wait until January; the sun will not fall out of the sky.

ORDERING SEEDS If you're planning lots of seed-sowing next year, particularly special vegetable varieties, then get online immediately and order your seeds before anyone else.

BRUSHING AWAY SNOW Definitely make sure that shrubs aren't weighed down with too much snow because they can break under the strain, so get out there and brush it off periodically.

PRUNING FRUIT TREES If you have inherited fruit trees that have seen better days, then December and January are the best times to get them pruned, for a better look and/or for higher yield. Always go for a recommended tree surgeon or get references before you let anyone near your trees.

BEING WELCOMING A bit of house-decorating is essential at this time of year, and it needn't be taxing or take forever. A wreath (or just a spray of foliage) for your door (see page 226) and a cheerful, five-minute window-box makeover (see page 137) will make things jolly both for you and for passers-by.

RETREATING INDOORS In the following pages, you'll find ideas for Christmas decorations and indoor gardening to keep your green fingers happy while it's frightful outside.

Sugared fruit for the table

It's unashamedly girly, but I love the look of this, and it's an easy, cheap way of making things look really special. Personally, I would class this fruit as totally edible, but be aware that the 'glue' is raw egg whites, and for this reason it's officially just for decoration. You can circumvent this and have peace of mind by sourcing something called 'meringue powder', which is sold in special cake shops and which has been pasteurised ... up to you. Either way, it's a crying shame not to have the option of gobbling this lovely fruit up eventually.

YOU WILL NEED **Small, pretty pieces of fruit** Mini pears are perfect, or cherries, figs, small apples, bunches of grapes, clementines, tangerines – you choose.
Egg white or meringue powder
A soft paintbrush or pastry brush
Caster sugar
Waxed paper

METHOD Wash and dry all the fruit carefully. Try to keep stems intact – they're very useful for holding the fruit and look lovely too.

Lightly whisk the egg white or make up the meringue powder and start painting your fruit. It's best to do this in batches, say four or five pieces at a time. Place the painted fruit carefully on a sheet of waxed paper and give them five minutes or so to dry a little, because if the egg white is too wet then the sugar just dissolves into it.

Finally, sieve a cloud of sugar over your tacky fruit to cover it completely. If you're a perfectionist, you'll wait for the fruit to dry and cover the bits you couldn't get to afterwards. When everything is dry, you can arrange the fruit in bowls or saucers. I often give these as presents – if you put them in a gorgeous box, it's better than getting designer chocolates (and far healthier).

A five-minute Christmas door

I think the whole idea of a wreath can seem a bit too much like hard work sometimes, particularly in the run-up to Christmas. In this case, it might be worth knowing that one of the nicest things you can do to a door at Christmas is to gather together a bunch of festive foliage, tie it with a ribbon and hang it, upside down, from your door or overhead, as you would with mistletoe. I got everything for this either from the garden or the local park. Whether you live in the city or the sticks, have a garden or not, there is an abundance of wreath-material out there if you ask for it. There is only one rule, and that is to go for evergreen foliage. It doesn't need to be fancy, it just needs to be tough enough to look good for three weeks or so hanging on your door.

YOU WILL NEED

Foliage Here are a few suggestions; mix them up or stay pure, it's up to you.
Ivy: in my eyes, perfection.
Holly: a classic for Christmas and ubiquitous too. If you can find variegated holly, then you've lucked out because it looks gorgeous.
Conifers: this forms the basis of most bought wreaths and can be very pretty, particularly if you can find something with nice fat silvery leaves.
Herbs: rosemary, bay and sage make brilliant wreath material and smell yummy too. Many people have a rosemary bush in their garden.
Eucalyptus: if you or a neighbour has a tree, then ask to pilfer some of this beautiful foliage.
Camellia: if you're lucky enough to have access to lots of this, then go for it – makes a very smart, sexy wreath.
Viburnum tinus: slightly dull leaves, but lovely, honey-scented flowers make up for it. Again, this is fairly ubiquitous, especially in urban environments.
Sharp secateurs
Garden twine
Some beautiful ribbon

METHOD To make this cheat's wreath, gather together your greenery, cleaning up the stems as you go so that the bottom 10cm are stripped of leaves and flowers. You are aiming for a large, flat-ish shape with a good 'side', as this is going to be hung upside down on your door. Keep things quite long and straggly because generosity rather than neatness is the order of the day. This is not the kind of deal where you can start poking in flowers and dried fruit (for that, you really do need a proper wreath, and there are instructions below for one of these). When you're happy with your bunch, tie it together really tightly with garden twine, snip the ends so they are neat, and cover the twine with silken ribbon. Hang it from your door (I tap in a small nail and hook the ribbon over it).

MORE If you want to make a proper wreath, here's how. First, you need a wreath form, which you can either buy from a florist or make yourself from heavy-duty green wire. To attach the greenery, start by gathering together small bunches of it, about 10–15cm long and wiring them together with thin wire. Once you've made enough (and you always need more than you think), simply attach them to your wreath form, one by one, using a long length of wire. It's fiddly at first, but easy once you get the hang of it. Now all you need do is add any fancy bits, like rosehips, berries, dried fruit, nuts or pinecones – that crafting staple, a glue-gun comes in useful here. I could go on, and I must stress that the options when it comes to wreathery are far, far broader than this. A simple circle of twigs, lavish and thicket-like, with birds or flowers poking through, or minimalist and Blair-Witchy with a rosehip or two, are equally delightful … as with everything, the choice is entirely yours.

Candle pots for the table

These are incredibly simple to make and hugely useful as decoration over Christmas. They can be displayed on their own or alongside other plants, on a mantelpiece or table.

YOU WILL NEED

A thick plastic bag

Scissors

One small terracotta pot 15cm diameter is nice.

A block of oasis foam Available from big garden centres and florists. Soak in water for an hour or so to ensure it's fully saturated.

One candle I like quite thick, church-type candles.

A packet of toothpicks

Sticky tape

Foraged greenery Anything you like, really, as long as it is evergreen and looks gorgeous.

METHOD

Cut out a square of plastic from the bag and shove it into the bottom of your pot to cover the drainage hole and stop any water seeping out. Now cut some oasis off the block so that when you stuff it in the pot, it stands proud of the top by a few centimetres. You don't need it to be the right shape – square is just fine.

Prepare your candle by firmly taping some toothpicks around the bottom of it so that you can eventually stick the thing into the middle of the oasis and it is in no danger of toppling over.

With your candle stuck in the oasis, have a lovely time sticking small pieces of ivy, or whatever other greenery you've found, around it until it's completely covered and looks super-pretty.

That's it. You can, of course, also add flowers here if you want, or berries, rosehips … there are no rules.

Hippeastrum for a post-Christmas lift

These beautiful, gigantic bulbs are usually sold in autumn for flowering over Christmas. They look wonderfully festive with their bold, bright colours and thick, fleshy petals, but being a paperwhite narcissi devotee, I prefer to postpone my *Hippeastrum* moment (for a 'moment' it certainly is) until December, when I can snap up bulbs that have been left over and languishing in the shops and are often considerably reduced in price as a result. This means I can get lots, and I think that profusion is key here, for although one *Hippeastrum* can look striking on its own, a group of them all in their own pots, or in one large container, can be quite breathtaking.

Hippeastrum hybrids are often incorrectly sold as 'amaryllis' (which is actually a separate genus with its own loveliness) – so be aware that they may be labelled with either name. These plants originate from Central and South America where they live on rocky hillsides at various different altitudes – but that is just an interesting factoid, really, because these man-made hybrids are bred specifically for growing in pots, making them a far cry from their hillside cousins. They flower from winter to spring and will not tolerate frost, but can take low light levels, which makes them perfect for the house.

YOU WILL NEED

***Hippeastrum* bulbs** As many as you can afford. It's lovely to have a mixture of colours and heights too. Often, you'll see the beginnings of green leaves protruding from the top of the bulb, but not always. Just remember that the end with the spindly, dry roots is the bottom of the bulb.

A large bowl for soaking

Pots You can either plant them all together in one large container, or do as I do and give yourself more flexibility for 'arranging' and put each one in its own pot. For this purpose, bear in mind that a large bulb needs a pot a little larger than its diameter. As long as there is some depth for the roots to grow down, this plant will be happy, so it's worth finding a pot that I would describe as a 'mini long-tom', which is tall and narrow; the same proportions as a pot you might grow lilies in is perfect. Mine are roughly 15cm diameter and 25cm high.

Compost A mixture of two-thirds John Innes No. 2 and one-third multi-purpose.

METHOD

Buying *Hippeastrum* in December can be a bit like a lucky dip. You won't get the pick of the bunch, but there's a joy in getting the leftovers and bringing them to life. Just because a bulb is all on its own on a shelf looking sad doesn't mean it's not viable: I often find the unwanted plants are the less rare ones and thus the cheapest and best growers.

Once you get the bulbs home, fill a large bowl with luke-warm water and put your bulbs in to soak, because they'll be very dry and brittle and almost in a coma at this stage. A good soak for a couple of hours will send the message that it's time to wake up and start growing.

Now prepare your growing medium, mixing John Innes No. 2 and multi-purpose compost, two-thirds to one-third, in a trug. If you're happy to use just John Innes No. 2, then dispense with the multi-purpose altogether. I only add it here because, if I'm doing lots of pots, it makes things a bit lighter, both weight-wise and economically.

Once your bulbs have had their soak, you can plant them, roots-down. Unlike other bulbs, which you bury, these need to be only half-submerged in the compost, so fill your pots until they're almost full, then gently place the bulb on top and firm in some more compost around it, so that the surface of the compost stops at the fattest part of the bulb.

All that's needed now is for you to water the whole thing, until you see water coming out of the hole at the bottom of the pot, and leave them inside on a saucer or tray in a cool, bright place, like an unheated spare room by a window or a sheltered porch. If the weather is unseasonably fine, then they can go outside, but remember that they will not tolerate frost, so bring them in at night to be safe. Keep them watered.

The time it takes to flower depends on the conditions and variety, but the speed (a few weeks) always leaves me breathless, especially knowing that this emerald sword reaching for the sky comes from such a crinkly, brown piece of stuff.

Most people throw away their bulbs and start again next year, but they are actually quite easy to get going again if you have the space to store them whilst they're dormant. When flowering is over and the stem starts to wither, reduce the watering so it's basically dry most of the time, with just an occasional moistening. Keep it outside over the summer, in this dry state, and then move it indoors again as soon as any frost threatens, keeping it dry until you want to get it going again. For this second and any subsequent flowerings, I would advise carefully replacing the compost, and using a weak solution of tomato food once a week to give it an extra boost.

MORE I often cover the tops of the bulbs and the compost with a generous helping of sphagnum moss, which can look particularly gorgeous if you're planting lots of bulbs in one container. In addition, because they are so long-lasting, *Hippeastrum* make the most fabulous presents – whether they're in flower or not.

Turn over for pictures

January

I suppose it is a function of the human psyche – optimists as we are – to label what is essentially mid-winter as the beginning of the year. It allows us to look at things with new eyes and a sense of reinvigoration – it allows us to hope. An ingenious construct this, because at first glance nature seems to have given up the ghost at this time of year. The garden sits there as if in a coma, and when I go outside at the end of my first year, it's not the dead, brittle stems or the bare patches that surprise me, but the stillness. Only a few short months ago, these flowerbeds were a billowing sea of crazy colour; even the lawn was dotted with drops of dandelion sunshine. It all seems like a distant memory now, but I'm not disheartened because in this one area of my life, I have thought ahead and planted all my favourite winter-flowering plants to get me through the darkness.

It's not perceptible from a distance, but as soon as I get close I remember that my garden is still full of jewels that I planted back in March and April just for this purpose. The wintersweet (*Chimonanthus praecox*) is doing its thing, pumping out sweet, intoxicating scent from its funny waxy, claw-like flowers, and the delicate pale yellow flowers of my favourite, delicious winter-flowering honeysuckle (*Lonicera* x *purpusii* 'Winter Beauty') are unfurling with their fresh, floral perfume. My two precious daphnes (*Daphne odora* 'Aureomarginata'), which were wince-makingly expensive when I bought them, have thick pink buds which are already giving heavenly scent, making them seem like the bargain of my life.

The very best of my scented miracle plants, the *Sarcococca confusa* with which I have liberally peppered the garden and my front door, are bursting into life (see page 240) and giving me that warm sweetshop smell that is so welcome on a cold day. I have enough of this to cut sprigs off it and scent the entire house, including the loo … it's hard to be glum when your house smells of bonbons.

And there's so much more; my hyacinths are up and blooming (see page 174), there are crocuses peeping out of pots (see page 120), and snowdrops appearing which I had quite forgotten about. The *Violas* I put in containers and window-boxes months ago are still going strong, even though I have long since ceased to deadhead them (see page 178); there are daffodils appearing; and, yes, my tulips and alliums are shyly breaking the surface. And despite the bitter cold I can see tiny new shoots and thick juicy buds all over the flowerbeds; the garden might have looked like it was sleeping, but it was only pretending.

WHAT TO DO IN YOUR VIRGIN GARDEN THIS MONTH

A LITTLE LIGHT CLEARING This is a great time to steal a march on weeds (yes, they grow even over the winter) and get ready for spring. Wait for a mild day and get in there with a trowel to catch anything you recognise as unwelcome. Don't be too hectic about it, though, because some of those little green leaves may be the self-seeded babies of plants that you love and want more of. Now is also a good time to cut back your perennial plants and do a general tidy-up. If you don't do it now, it'll be March before you know it and cutting out the dead stuff without damaging the new growth emerging underneath will be tricky. Likewise, you can prune shrubs that look like they need a better shape (but always refer to a book or the internet before you go a-chopping).

PLANTING THE VERY LAST BULBS If you haven't planted any bulbs yet, then there's still time to whack in some tulips, which will make your spring and early summer extra-special.

SOME CLEANING If you haven't already done so, then this 'hiatus' is a good moment to finish any tidying and get your pots washed and your tools tidied. Tidying and new year go hand in hand and it will feel good to go out in the chilly air and do something constructive.

PUTTING UP SUPPORTS Whilst the garden is at a low ebb, it's an easy time to put up or improve supports at the back of borders for climbing plants. If you've got brick walls, then vine-eyes are a quick fix as you can bang them into the mortar with a hammer, but if there's time, get a drill out (see page 33) and use screws as these will last longer.

PRUNING VINES If you've got ivy, Virginia creeper, or climbing hydrangea growing up your house walls, then this is the time to cut them back. You can hack away at these quite gaily to keep them away from doors and windows – they will be fine.

RECYCLING YOUR CHRISTMAS TREE If you've got a large garden, then you can cut up your old Christmas tree into pieces and spread them out (at the back of borders is perfect). Otherwise, use your local council's disposal service. You can also use the trunk to make a bee house by chopping it up into short pieces, placing them in an old wooden box and drilling holes of different sizes, but no larger than 10mm diameter, into the cut ends, making sure you don't drill all the way through to the other side. Ensure that the holes are free of sawdust and splinters. If you place this box somewhere sunny, sheltered, and off the ground, solitary bees may well find it and start using the holes to make their nests, and that's good for them and your garden.

Sarcococca on your doorstep

This is really just a eulogy for one of my favourite plants. Imagine a plant that has the smartest, most elegant shiny green leaves. Imagine that this shiny green, leafy plant is evergreen and could cope with shade – even the dry shade that you might find under a tree, or in a pot under the porch of someone who's not altogether regular when it comes to watering. Now imagine (as if that weren't enough) that this plant has the loveliest, prettiest, tiniest white flowers that let out the most intoxicatingly sweet scent for weeks on end – amazing, right? But that's not the best bit. The best bit is that those flowers, with that scent, will come out to delight you at the darkest, coldest time of year.

This is a must-have plant. I remember when it was first pointed out to me by an expert gardener one summer, I didn't look twice, and then I came across it again the following winter. This time it was spewing out its fabulous scent and I duly sat up and took notice. I have *Sarcococca* dotted all over the garden, but for me, the best place to have it is in pots by the front door as a permanent and welcoming fixture throughout the winter. There are various different forms; I love the one called *Sarcococca hookeriana* var. *digyna* because it has longer-than-average leaves and beautiful reddish stems, and the anthers of the flowers are flushed with pink. But unless you're a real details person, the common *Sarcococca confusa* looks much the same.

YOU WILL NEED
1 *Sarcococca* plant You can get these in various sizes all year round. It's fine to plant it in a large container, even if it's a small plant, because it will eventually grow into its space. If it looks lonely you could surround it with some cyclamen, or small ivy.
A container to plant it in My plants are happy and producing loads of blooms in a deep pot 30cm x 37cm.
A saucer for your pot
Compost I use my half-and-half mix of multi-purpose and John Innes No. 2, with a handful of food granules mixed in and some water-retaining gel (for quantities, read the instructions on the packet).

METHOD
Half-fill the pot with the compost mix, remove the plant from its plastic, and muss up the roots a little so they know it's okay to roam outwards. The top of the plant's compost should lie just a few centimetres shy of the rim of the pot. Fill in around the edges with more compost, until it's all snug and flat at the top, then put it just outside your front door, and water the whole thing well.

It should be about to flower now, so enjoy the sweet scent and marvel at it, but don't forget about it afterwards. Just because this plant is brilliant and will cope with a lot, it doesn't mean it won't appreciate regular watering. Because this is a permanent planting, I remove the top 5cm of compost every year in springtime and replace it with new, mixed in the same way as before.

MORE   Just a tiny sprig of this will scent a whole room for days. Simply cut it, put it in a small vase by your bed and dream sweetly. If you're short on space by your front door, then it's perfectly okay to plonk your plant in a tall, narrow container (like an old chimney pot or similar) and train it so that it grows up against a wall. Just put up some wires or trellis and gently tie the stems in so they are flat against the wall and prune off any that are in your way.

Radishes for the ultimate sandwich

Not being wholly wedded to self-sufficiency, I find there's too much going on in the busy spring and summer months for me to think about radishes, so I like to sow them indoors in mid-winter when I'm longing to look at new shoots. Radishes (*Raphanus sativus*) are thought to come originally from China and have been delighting palates (or not) for thousands of years. There are a huge variety of different types available from seed. Being a member of the mustard family, the leaves are also edible and delicious, particularly as microgreens (see page 192).

YOU WILL NEED

Radish seeds Try anything that takes your fancy. I've never had a radish I didn't like, so I'm not fussed about variety for taste, but there are some gorgeous colours out there, like 'Pink Beauty' or 'Cherry Belle', and of course the sexiest radish of all is the elongated 'French Breakfast', which the French eat with butter and a sprinkling of salt (how I yearn to be that chic).
A container that fits inside your window-sill Imagine a radish and make sure your tray or pot is deeper than this.
Multi-purpose compost
A pencil or dibber

METHOD

It couldn't be easier. Simply fill your container with compost, and water it well by plunging it into another tray of water. Then make some lines in the compost with a pencil or dibber, and sow the seeds very thinly in this little furrow – ideally about a centimetre apart. Press the compost gently back into place over the seeds, put the lid over your tray or use a plastic bag to cover if you are using a pot. You want to create a bit of humidity, like in a greenhouse, for the seeds to germinate.

Once you see signs of life (which will be soon), remove the cover and watch your little darlings grow. If you have sown thinly, then you shouldn't need to thin them out, but if you see that there are two or more seedlings all squished into one tiny area, then very carefully remove all but one of them. I often do this by simply cutting the leaves off above the compost with scissors so that I don't disturb the roots of the one I've chosen to grow on. Keep an eye on your radishes, watering them regularly, and they should be ready for eating within four to six weeks.

If you're not a fan of munching on a radish alone, then layer sliced radishes inside two slices of really good, very generously buttered, toffee-like brown bread. I often add Marmite, but it's okay, you don't have to.

Fat balls for the birds

Fat balls are an effective way of delivering nutrition and much-needed calories to birds during the cold months. There is masses of conflicting advice about which nuts, seeds and fruit are safe for different birds, along with various worrying information about some nuts being positively dangerous for them, so I find the easiest way to get a good mix is to use a packet of ready-mixed birdseed for small birds. These packets are available year-round in garden centres, DIY stores and pet shops, and I usually buy one that's approved by the RSPB or similar. Having said this, there is nothing to stop you using your common sense (and your leftovers) and trying a range of stuff in your fat balls, including small pea-sized pieces of stale bread, cooked bacon and dried fruit, if you have the space and inclination to collect enough scraps.

YOU WILL NEED

Some fat I use a block of ordinary lard, but beef suet works too.
Some birdseed (See above.)
Some means of delivering your goodies To hang the balls from a tree, some people use a mesh bag, like the stuff you buy lemons and tangerines in, but there's talk of beaks and claws getting stuck in them, so I just use garden string (see below). If that's a bit fiddly for you, then a simple shallow container, like a terracotta or plastic pot saucer is fine too. You can also buy feeders designed to contain fat balls.
String

METHOD

Measure out the ingredients so that the amount of fat is double that of the birdseed or scraps. So, for example, if you are using 200g of birdseed, then you'll need 400g of lard. Melt the fat in a saucepan so it's just liquid (you don't need it bubbling). Then remove it from the heat and mix in the seeds and nuts. The mixture should be thick and clumpy enough to squidge together into balls. Cover with cling film and leave in the fridge or outside to harden. Then take a long piece of string and wrap it around the ball as if you were wrapping a parcel. Secure it tightly at the top with a knot and hang it from a tree with more string. If you've tied it tight enough, the fat ball sort of 'sticks' to the string and doesn't fall off as it gets smaller. You can hang these on a tree and they look like Christmas baubles, with the added benefit that they attract sweet little birds, rather than huge, brutish ones.

Alternatively, you can put the balls straight into a wire bird-feeder if you have one, or simply squish the mixture into a saucer and leave it on your window-sill, making sure it's secured, because the birds will perch on its rim.

A hanging hellebore

Helleborus x *hybridus* has been deeply fashionable for many years now, and it's easy to see why. They flower for months and their leaves are evergreen and they have downward-facing flowers in wonderfully soft shades. These amazing colour permutations are the result of human hybridisation (hence the 'x' in the name). When I was new to gardening, and having to fit all my plants into containers on my balcony, I bought one and planted it in a hanging basket so that I could get a good view of those shy, nodding blooms from below. Had I read anything about hellebores before I committed this act of hanging basketry (tales of moisture, shade and richness-loving), I would never have attempted it. But years later, that same hellebore is still going strong in its original basket. I've been hideously neglectful, often forgetting to water it, and I've certainly never added new compost, and it's still absolutely fine in its new home hanging on the branch of my apple tree.

YOU WILL NEED
1 *Helleborus* x *hybridus* plant These are coming on sale now in garden centres, but it's well worth seeking out specialist nurseries online who will provide the widest and most delectable choice.
1 hanging basket Mine is a standard 35cm diameter.
Compost I use a half-and-half mixture of ordinary peat-free multi-purpose and John Innes No. 2.
Water-retaining granules
Fertiliser granules
An empty pot

METHOD
First, water your hellebore thoroughly in its pot by soaking it in a tray or bucket of water for half an hour or so. Make sure that the lining of your hanging basket has holes in it (some don't). If not, then cut some by making a few nicks in the plastic with scissors.

Next, mix the compost with your water-retaining granules and fertiliser in the quantities stipulated on the packet. Fill your basket 10cm shy of the rim and water the whole thing, standing it on an empty pot to keep it level. This pre-watering will give the water-retaining granules a chance to expand before you plant your hellebore.

Now remove your plant from its plastic, rubbing the roots gently to let them know it's okay to spread out, and plant it firmly in the basket, adding more compost if you need to, but leaving a good couple of centimetres between the top of the compost and the rim of the basket for watering purposes.

Water the whole thing again, making sure that the basket and its contents are saturated and then hang it up, preferably on the branch of a tree or somewhere out of the sun, in order to replicate that woodland feel.

MORE   You can pick the blooms and float them in bowls for the perfect winter table (see overleaf). You can of course use other types of hellebore for this project, but check the label and stick to those with an eventual height and spread of 45cm maximum; anything bigger won't be happy in your basket.

February

It feels like winter is never going to end and for me, this is the culmination of the year proper, when frosty, spiky hardness has reached its peak and slowly, almost imperceptibly starts to succumb to warmth and that soft, yolky egginess of March and Easter beyond. But this time is, for some plants, their moment to shine; I'm talking particularly of all the early bulbs that were peeping through the soil last month and are now up and singing. I planted lots of my favourite *Iris reticulata* in the autumn, both in pots and in the ground. These are tiny, upright things with the most delicate of petals and colours from the brightest cobalt ('Cantab') to the sexiest, subtlest of greys ('Katharine Hodgkin'). I pick all of them as soon as they appear in bud, bring them into the warmth of the house in little vases and watch as each one opens with a pop.

The violets are making me swoon too. I had a huge collection in pots, which I planted into the ground when I arrived and they seem to love their new home. They are also Jemima's favourite flower and she drags me outdoors to pick little fistfuls of them. The scent is so unbelievably special, sweet and earthy all at once, but with the kind of punch that eventually numbs your olfactory senses. They too go in tiny vases and, when I am feeling particularly goddessy, get crystalised to go on top of cakes.

A visit to any garden at this time of year always reminds me that I need more snowdrops and *Cyclamen coum* (a tiny, fat-leaved cyclamen that flowers right now, and the prettiest of them all I think). The other star of the show is the winter aconite (*Eranthis hyemalis*) which carpets the ground with bright yellow flowers, each with its own frilly ruff of leaves. The hippeastrums are emerging from their beautiful buds (see page 232) and there are daffodils in abundance everywhere.

Because I can feel spring in my bones, there's potato chitting to be done (see page 258) as well as the planting of some special things (snowdrops and a gooseberry bush) that I ordered way back when, but the biggest job this month has been to admire the hellebores, which I am growing both in hanging baskets in The Apple Garden and in window-boxes. I float them in bowls and get lost in speckled-petalled thoughts of the gardening year ahead.

It seems strange to end this first year with the chopping of a tree, but that is just what happened. One of the two apple trees in The Apple Garden never blossomed and yielded just one solitary fruit. Had it been the only apple tree, I would have kept it, but since I had two, down it came and its removal opened up a view that I now couldn't live without.

WHAT TO DO IN YOUR VIRGIN GARDEN THIS MONTH

PLANNING YOUR NEW PROJECTS — If you're itching to get sowing seeds, then get yourself ready for this by buying a propagator and washing out and sterilising little pots and seed trays. The golden rule is not to do too much, because tiny seeds become huge plants, so make sure you not only have room to plant out everything you sow, but also that you have the space to nurture it from seed-hood until planting out time.

INSTALLING A COLD FRAME — If you think you're going to be a seed-sower, then it's well worth buying or making a cold frame. A cold frame is basically a mini-greenhouse where you can keep plants in some degree of shelter but still give them the light they need to be healthy. There are lots available – the one I bought was very cheap and is falling apart, so if you're going to invest in one, well, all I can say is that you get what you pay for.

ORDERING PLUG PLANTS — In order to avoid overcrowding and your terrace starting to look like a nursery, it's well worth complementing your seed-sowing with plug plants which will be sent to you when they're ready for planting. This cuts out the need for nurturing tiny seeds and is much, much cheaper than buying larger plants.

GETTING AHEAD OF THE GAME — A little light weeding this month will pay real dividends later in the year, and it'll make you feel deeply virtuous too. It's much easier to do now than later as well, because you can see them clearly.

DEADHEADING — Keep your winter pots looking fabulous by removing the flowers one by one as they go over. This will also prolong the life of the display.

GETTING NOSY — This is one of the best times in the year to visit gardens because you get an insight into the design without being distracted by masses of gorgeous flowers, and you get to see how the experts maintain loveliness throughout the winter. There is also hardly anybody else about, which is heaven.

PRUNING — You can get going with your clematis (see page 58) and wisteria (see page 100) now if you have them and have a good look around the garden to see if there is anything dead or dying that needs removing from your other shrubs.

Quick topiary for Valentine's Day

Roses are delightful and gorgeous but unless you live somewhere impossibly sexy like Colombia, your Valentine's rose bouquet will have had to be flown to you from a faraway land. Here's a fun, easy valentine's present that can be a permanent thing on your terrace or window-sill, or perched somewhere in the garden. The ivy will eventually grow to make a heart ... hopefully mirroring your relationship. Quick topiary, or 'false topiary' is an impatient person's dream. With this method, you can use ivy or other evergreen climbers to create pots of dense greenery in lots of different shapes (silly or sensible). My heart shape here is basically two-dimensional but you can buy frames or make your own for globes or cones or whatever tickles your fancy.

YOU WILL NEED

A small pot of small-leaved ivy Widely available from garden centres.
A wire coat-hanger
Some pliers
A pot About 20cm diameter.
Compost I use half John Innes No. 2 and half multi-purpose compost.
Fertiliser granules

METHOD First you need to make your frame. To do this, use your pliers to un-bend the hook bit of the coat-hanger, then un-twist the 'neck' of it and then straighten all the bends so that you are left with a long, slightly squiffy piece of wire. Now grab the wire at each end and bring them together, twisting these ends together with the pliers, so that you have a 'stalk' about 7cm long to poke into the soil. Hold the stalk between your knees and shape the rest into a rough heart shape – it doesn't have to be perfect (if it is, then your lover will expect you to be perfect too and that's never a good thing).

Put your creation aside for a second while you mix the compost and a spoonful of fertiliser granules, and fill your pot so there's a two-centimetre gap between the top of the pot and the top of the compost. Firm it down gently. Now remove your ivy plant from its plastic pot and plant it firmly. You are going to stick your frame bang in the centre of the pot so you need to plant your ivy just in front of where the frame will go.

Gently spread out the tendrils, and start twisting them round the bottom of the frame. If they don't stick, then tie them in with a bit of string. As the plant grows, just keep twisting the tendrils around each other and the frame, until it is completely covered. You can prune out any that you don't need. Keep the pot watered and every year remove the top three centimetres of compost and replace it with new.

Sowing basil

Having had trouble with growing basil from seed in the past, the discovery that I could divide a bought pot of supermarket basil quite easily and get all the floppy green leaves I wanted stopped me from trying again. But crazy stuff happens, and in the midst of getting ready to move house, I came across a forgotten packet of seed and decided to give it another go. This time it worked beautifully. I have since tried again twice more, just to make sure it wasn't a fluke, and it isn't. I still have my pots of divided basil which I use for cooking, but sowing my own means that I can have something that looks lovely on a table too, for people to pick their own. You can sow basil indoors any time of the year. The rate of growth will be affected by light levels though, so if you like speed, then do this as the days get longer.

YOU WILL NEED

A packet of basil seed
A terracotta pot I like to use a shallow pot with its own saucer.
Some seed compost This can be either ready-made or you can mix multi-purpose with a handful of horticultural grit.
A sieve with big holes For making fine compost.
A squirty bottle One that emits a fine mist.

METHOD

Fill your pot with seed compost and tap it down gently, so that there is a centimetre or so between the top of the pot and the surface of the compost. Water the compost by leaving the whole pot to soak in a tray of water until you can see the surface glistening. Now scatter your seeds thinly on the surface of the damp compost so that there is a seed roughly every half-centimetre. It's impossible to be accurate about this so don't even try; I just give it as a guide so you know what 'scatter thinly' means.

Now cover the seeds with about half a centimetre of sieved compost and firm it down gently with your palm. Dampen the top layer of compost with a squirter and put the whole thing inside your kitchen window-sill or somewhere similar. Be patient and remember to keep the compost moist.

When the little seedlings appear, and once you've got over your delight, let them grow on, thinning them out by pinching out the weaker-looking seedlings if you see two or more plants squashed together in the same bit of earth. This is a wonderful opportunity to taste the leaves at different stages of growth. You may find that baby basil leaves are your desert island food, in which case sow some more immediately, this time in a shallower, wider pot, and keep sowing them in succession to provide you with your fix. Otherwise, start harvesting as soon as each plant has six to eight leaves by pinching the stalk just above a new pair of leaves.

MORE I have yet to grow such a glut of home-sown basil that I would dare to toss handfuls of leaves in a whizzer and make pesto. I still harvest with the same kind of reverence that normal people (not Alexis Colby) have for caviar. But in case you've grown masses and masses of wonderful leaves, here is the ultimate pesto recipe. Whizz two chopped cloves of garlic and two large cups of basil leaves into a paste, then add 50g of pinenuts, 50g of Parmesan cheese and 150ml of best olive oil.

New potatoes in a pot

This is one of the easiest edibles I've ever grown in a pot and I can't think why it took me so long to try it. Potatoes (*Solanum tuberosum*) belong to the same genus that gives us aubergines (see page 80) and many beautiful ornamentals. The flowers are gratifyingly easy to spot, being often star-like, with five petals and pronounced bright yellow centres. Unless you've got loads and loads of space and you really like potatoes, I would seriously advise you to stick to new potatoes (i.e. early ones, that you harvest in early or midsummer) rather than the big maincrop ones. The reason is that earlies suffer less from diseases borne by warm weather, and they are also (I think) rather more delicious. The other reason is that new potatoes are expensive to buy in the shops, and maincrop ones aren't.

This method is for one pot of 33cm diameter, into which you will plant four seed potatoes, yielding about 20 potatoes in total. If that's not enough for you, then get more pots and double or triple up as necessary. The leaves look perfectly lovely as they grow, so if you've got two or three of them on a terrace it's not going to be an eyesore.

YOU WILL NEED

Seed potatoes These are available right now. Variety is a personal thing, but my favourite has always been Charlotte, so that is the one I go for.
An empty egg box This isn't strictly necessary, but it's perfect for keeping your seed potatoes upright whilst they're chitting (see below).
A large pot Mine is 33cm diameter, and terracotta. The more capacious the container, the better, and in fact, there are plenty of people who grow their potatoes in big plastic bags or stacks of tyres. Call me old-fashioned, but I prefer something a little prettier.
Multi-purpose compost

METHOD When you get your seed potatoes, they'll have lots of small nodules on them. These are the beginnings of shoots, and in order to get them growing, you need to expose them to a bit of warmth and a bit of light. For this, put each little potato into its own compartment of your egg box, making sure that the largest shoot is uppermost, and place the whole thing inside your kitchen window-sill. This is called 'chitting'.

Over the next few weeks, the shoots will slowly swell and stretch. They end up looking like tiny, hairy pineapples (sort of). There are varying thoughts about how big your shoots (or 'eyes') have to be before planting, but the general consensus is that you should wait until they are about 2.5cm long, and you should reckon on this taking six to eight weeks. If you start the process at the beginning of February, then your potatoes should be ready to plant as we begin to say goodbye to frost. You should be careful though, and always delay planting until you're sure you're ready to take the chance. Luckily, pots are moveable, and if a frosty night is forecast, you can move it somewhere out of danger – inside a shed or a garage, or even in the house if necessary.

To plant your chitted potatoes, fill your pot with 10cm of compost and carefully place four potatoes, evenly spaced, on the surface, shoots facing skywards. Cover these gently with another 10cm of compost and water it well. The leaves should appear gratifyingly quickly (mine took just over two weeks to show themselves). Keep watering and wait until the leaves are about 15cm high, at which point carefully cover the whole lot again with more compost, so that there's only 5cm of leaf showing. Repeat this 'earthing up' process once more until you reach the top of the pot, at which point you can sit back and enjoy the beautiful foliage, making sure the pot is watered regularly.

You know your potatoes are ready to pull when you see flowers. Make sure you gather an audience around you for this momentous event, for there is little to beat the magic of one potato becoming many.

I'm not going to tell you how to eat new potatoes – everyone knows they should be boiled and eaten, slightly cold, with lashings of chopped mint.

A wigwam of peas for picnicking

Simply the most delicious raw food you can eat – a wigwam of peas in the garden is tantamount to having your very own bonbon tree. I've never met anyone who doesn't love fresh peas straight from the pod. You can grow them in containers too, providing support of course. Getting early peas is slightly more complicated than later ones because you have to sow them indoors rather than directly into the ground, but for the sake of avoiding grief, it's better to grow early peas because later ones often fall victim to pea moth, whose spawn tend to start munching in midsummer. If you don't want to sow, then wait a few weeks and buy some ready-grown seedlings at the garden centre.

YOU WILL NEED

Pea seeds I love 'Kelvedon Wonder' because they're quick to grow but there are loads of varieties out there so be adventurous.

A deep modulated seed tray Alternatively, use some rootrainers with a plastic lid, or the insides of cardboard loo rolls to sow your peas in. Like sweet peas, they need a long, deep root run.

Pea sticks For support. I like to use hazel, which you can buy in bundles from good nurseries. They last for ages and look gorgeous. But three bamboo canes covered in pea netting would work too. Because early peas tend to be dwarf varieties, the support doesn't have to be too tall, but obviously read the seed packet for measurements.

Multi-purpose compost

An open, weed-free bit of flowerbed in full sun Stuck with your desired wigwam.

METHOD

First sow your peas by filling your modules, rootrainers or cardboard tubes with compost. Rootrainers or seed modules come with their own trays but if you're using loo roll insides, put them in a tray with sides so they're supported and you can sprinkle compost over the top. This always takes much longer than you think because you need to make sure each module is filled, and filled properly to the top. Keep tapping the tray on your work table to settle the compost and keep adding more until you're satisfied there aren't any air pockets in the modules. Push a pea into each module so it's buried about 2–3cm deep, cover them up and water them well. Now cover your tray with its lid. If you're using cardboard tubes, then you'll need to fashion a lid from a clear plastic bag, ensuring that the plastic is held away from the tops of the modules by poking a few chopsticks in amongst them.

Keep checking the seeds and as soon as most of the shoots have appeared, remove the covering. What needs to happen now is for the plants to develop a good root system but not too much top growth, so keep them as cool as possible, whilst giving them as much light as you can. I germinate the seeds inside my kitchen window-sill and then move them to a cold frame, but if you don't have one of these, then by the window in an unheated room is fine. Remember to keep the compost moist.

As soon as you see roots coming out of the bottom of the modules, pull one out and inspect the root system. If there's a good network of healthy-looking roots, they're ready for planting out. To do this, make a wigwam support out of pea sticks or bamboo and netting. Now dig a deep hole in the soil, next to a twig or cane of your wigwam, remove the plant from its module and plant it firmly, but with as little faffing around as possible with the roots. Plant at the same depth as it was previously in its module. If you've used loo rolls, then you can put the whole thing in without removing the cardboard – it will break down in the soil. Plant them 10cm apart.

The tendrils will start finding their support almost instantaneously and you should have your first peas around 12 weeks from sowing. Home-grown peas are so sweet and juicy that they are best eaten right then and there, straight from the pod and as quickly as possible. With every moment that passes between picking and eating, that sweetness diminishes, so don't even think of waiting.

SO, NOW WE ARE ONE

... and for the first time in my life, I can enjoy the anticipation of Year Two. It never worked that way when I was playing my happy game of musical chairs with pots on a balcony, because I was forever changing the structure. Here, I have literally, 'made my beds', planted them up and, yes, to a certain extent, I am committed – not because I can't move things about, but because I'm full of curiosity to see my garden develop. Box and bay topiary, mock orange (*Philadelphus*), lilac (*Syringa*) and of course, all the roses, to name but a few, are twelve months into their lives in this garden. They are its backbone: my special VIPs.

But it was the perennials (now hiding underground) and those delicious flash-in-the-pan annuals that gave me my perfect first summer, bravely and gorgeously doing their thing in my new space; filling what was for me a rather terrifying void with colour and scent in an inconceivably short time, and without bankrupting me in the process. Next year, I hope to replace the shed with something watertight, but other than that, I have absolutely no plans for the garden whatsoever, except to be in it, and enjoy it, and watch it grow. Thank you, sweet peas – see you next summer.

PLANTING PLAN TEMPLATES

Choosing what to plant in your virgin garden can be a bit daunting, so here are my suggestions if you don't feel like doing the whole thing yourself. I've devised the plans according to personality and mood, and laid them out to fit an average-sized flowerbed of 1 metre depth with a wall behind it. You can use the plans like wallpaper, simply repeating the design along your flowerbeds, or change the positions of the plants to suit your garden whatever shape it is. The key here is the combinations of plants, rather than the way I've laid them out.

The plants I've suggested will grow just fine in most 'ordinary' conditions, by which I mean moist but well-drained, slightly alkaline soil and a site that gets a good amount of sunshine throughout the day. This is not to say that they won't cope well in conditions other than this, but that if your site and soil are very special (i.e. very sandy, very clayey, very shady, very wet, acidic, or by the sea), then you should refer to your encyclopedia or talk to someone at your local nursery or garden centre and substitute my suggestions with similar-shaped plants that thrive in your particular conditions. These plans can be followed plant for plant, or just used as a springboard for inspiration – it's totally up to you.

I haven't included bulbs like tulips and daffodils here, or annual plants, but they should be added in every available empty space to keep your garden looking lovely as it matures. I've put suggestions for small trees with each plan, along with other suggestions to start you on your way to finding out what suits you.

Lastly, and most importantly, I've kept everything as low-maintenance as possible because we are always far, far busier than we think.

Planting plan for hopeless romantics

For all you soft-focus, Vaseline-on-the-lens wafty romantics out there.

1   Standard *Laurus nobilis* (bay) Beautiful and useful in equal measure.
2   *Hydrangea arborescens* 'Annabelle' Cloud-like blooms.
3   *Digitalis purpurea* (foxglove) Darkly romantic and mysterious all at once – and the bees will feast on it.
4   *Lavandula angustifolia* 'Hidcote' (lavender) The very best of all lavenders (in my humble opinion).
5   *Verbena bonariensis* (See page 124 for a eulogy.)
6   *Anemone hupehensis* 'Hadspen Abundance' (See also page 208.)
7   *Trachelospermum jasminoides* (star jasmine) A perfect, well-behaved climber, slow-growing but worth the wait, because it's evergreen, and the scent is amazing.

Suggestions and alternatives

Small tree *Amelanchier lamarckii* or *Magnolia stellata*
Other shrubs *Pittosporum tobira*, *Choisya* White Dazzler, *Cistus* x *corbariensis*
Other perennials Wafty: *Gaura lindheimeri* or malva. Spiky: *Verbascum* or delphinium.
Other climbers *Clematis armandii* or *Clematis montana*.

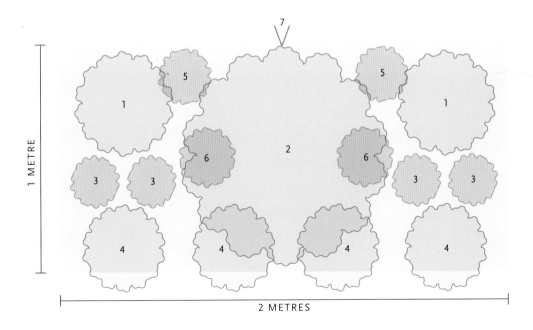

1 METRE

2 METRES

Planting plan for wild things

Wafty, wind-blown and edgy, for the Catherine Earnshaw or Heathcliff inside you.

1 *Rosa rugosa* (Hedgehog rose) Unbelievably pretty (and prickly) single rose with deep pink petals and yellow stamens. Comes in white (var. 'Alba'), paler pink (var. 'Rosea') and red (var. 'Rubra').
2 *Sarcococca hookeriana* var. *digyna* (Christmas box) Purple stems and a knock-out scent.
3 *Osmanthus x burkwoodii* An incredibly smart evergreen shrub with deliciously scented little white flowers in springtime – very good for training against a wall.
4 *Geranium* 'Johnson's Blue' The most intense and bluest of blues in profusion all summer long.
5 *Wisteria* (See page 100 for descriptions of different varieties.)

Suggestions and alternatives

Trees *Morus nigra* (black mulberry) or *Acer griseum* (paperbark maple)
Other shrubs *Rosa gallica*, *Choisya* 'Aztec Pearl'
Other perennials *Paeonia mlokosewitschii*, *Acanthus spinosus*, *Helleborus orientalis*, *Lychnis coronaria*, *Dicentra*, *Eryngium*
Other climbers *Hedera helix*, *Vitis coignetiae*

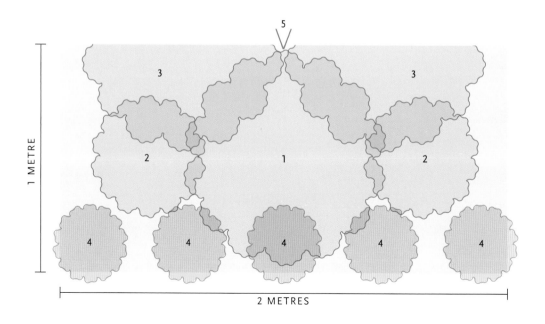

Planting plan for calm-seekers

Restful chic, for those with cluttered minds.

1 Standard *Viburnum tinus* Gorgeous, white, honey-scented flowers in spring, and it's incredibly tough too.
2 *Pittosporum tobira* 'Nanum' A smaller version, with smart, shiny evergreen leaves – makes a neat mound.
3 *Buxus sempervirens* (box) Little balls that you can either make yourself (see page 194) or buy ready-grown.
4 *Vinca minor* 'Gertrude Jekyll' One plant will cover about a square metre of ground. Little star-shaped white flowers.
5 *Hydrangea anomala* subsp. *petiolaris* A self-clinging climber that will lose its leaves but has beauteous, flaky bark to make up for it. Lovely white flowers in summer.

Suggestions and alternatives
Trees *Arbutus unedo, Prunus* x *subhirtella* 'Autumnalis'
Shrubs *Ilex aquifolium* (holly), *Laurus nobilis* (bay), *Myrtus communis* subsp. *tarentina* (myrtle)
Ground-cover *Epimedium, Hedera helix* 'Glacier' (for fast ground-cover) or 'Ivalace' (for slower)

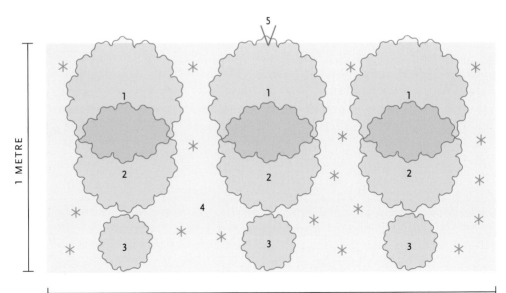

Glossary

ANNUAL A plant that flowers, sets seed and dies all in one year, like a sweet pea.

BARE-ROOT Trees or shrubs that are grown in a field, dug up, roots cleaned of earth and sent to you for planting. They're much cheaper to grow and lighter to transport than container-grown specimens, and that saving is passed on to you.

BEDDING Small plants that give you a temporary display over one season.

BIENNIAL A plant with a two-year life cycle. It grows its leaves and roots in the first year and flowers in the second, after which it sets seed and dies.

CHELSEA CHOP A method originally employed by nurserymen to reinvigorate perennials that were past their best. The plant is chopped back in late May to produce blooms later in the year.

CHITTING When seed potatoes are exposed to light and warmth for a little while before planting, they grow tiny, hairy shoots. The jury is out as to whether it's entirely necessary to chit potatoes, but it's hardly effortful, so I do.

CLOCHE Cloches come in different forms but they all give protection to plants. Bamboo ones stop young plants being trampled or pecked by birds, and plastic or glass cloches offer protection from cold or strong winds and invertebrates. They are widely available to buy, and it's easy to make little ones out of plastic bottles by simply cutting the end off and placing the small dome over your treasured seedling.

COLD FRAME An unheated mini-greenhouse that's perfect for housing plants that might suffer in an exposed position over the winter. You can control the air-flow by opening the lid to different degrees so that the plants become slowly acclimatised to the outside world. Widely available.

CORM A bit like a bulb, but technically a swollen stem. This doesn't matter in the least – just treat corms as you would bulbs.

CROCKS Broken pieces of pottery or polystyrene which I use to improve drainage in some of my containers. Some people use them in all containers but I use crocks only when I'm planting alpines or cacti which require very good drainage, or when I'm using 100 per cent loam-based compost which is very heavy and might block the hole at the bottom of my container.

CULTIVAR A plant that has been selected and bred by humans and then named. Cultivar names are always unitalicised and enclosed in quotation marks – for example, *Glechoma hederacea* 'Variegata'.

DEADHEAD When you remove flowers once they are past their best. This often helps the plant to produce more blooms.

DECIDUOUS A tree or shrub that loses its foliage in the winter.

DIVIDING When you dig up a perennial and chop it into bits to increase your stock.

EVERGREEN A tree, shrub or perennial that keeps its foliage all year round.

GENUS A group of plants that share general characteristics – the genus *Rosa* contains all the different roses in the whole world, and every name of every rose has to start with the word *Rosa*. The genus in a plant name always comes first, starts with a capital letter, and is always italicised.

GROUND-COVER Low-growing plants, usually evergreen, which will cover the ground, like ivy.

HERBACEOUS Describes soft-textured, non-woody plants that die back in winter; it is often added to the word 'perennial'.

HYBRID When plants are crossed (on purpose or otherwise), they produce hybrid offspring. Sometimes the characteristics of the parents merge to produce a really desirable plant. A hybrid is always denoted with an unitalicised 'x' between the two names, such as *Camellia* x *williamsii*.

LEAF CUTTING Some plants, like African violets or cape primroses, can reproduce by having their leaves cut and placed in a growing medium – this is a leaf cutting.

LEAF-MOULD This wonderful crumbly stuff is produced when leaves rot down. It's a good way to add nutrients to compost and improve its texture. I collect bags of leaves in the autumn, leave them to rot down for a year and then spread the leaf-mould on to the surface of the compost in my containers.

LONG-TOM POTS Extra-deep pots for growing tall bulbs, like lilies and anything that likes a deep root-run.

MICROGREENS Salad leaves harvested at infancy, like cress (but sexier).

MULCHING A mulch is anything that you spread on top of your soil to enrich it or to suppress weeds. Compost and manure are examples of soil-improving mulch and bark clippings or plastic sheeting are examples of weed-suppressing mulch. It's a good idea to mulch with something soil-improving whenever you can.

PEA STICKS Anything twiggy that can provide a climbing frame for peas or other climbing plants. I love willow and hazel ones, which are pretty widely available.

PERENNIAL A plant that sticks around year after year (as opposed to an annual which dies after one year). Sometimes a perennial's above-ground parts will die back in winter (see 'herbaceous' on page 277) and sometimes not.

PERLITE This stuff is actually volcanic glass. It is wonderful for raising seeds and cuttings because it is sterile and never gets soggy. I use it mixed with seed compost when I'm taking cuttings.

PLUG PLANTS Small plants, really, but at a very early stage and with hardly any soil. They are cheaper to buy in large numbers than more mature plants, and are a good option if you don't want to raise your own plants from seed.

'PREPARED' BULBS Bulbs that have been kept in cold storage to trick them into thinking they've been through winter and it's time to come out (even though that time may be Christmas).

ROOTSTOCK A root or part of a root used for grafting. Some trees, shrubs and climbers are reproduced by grafting, when you take a piece of root from one type of plant and attach a juvenile stem from another to it. Each piece is chosen for its desirable characteristics to produce a great plant. (See A wisteria tree on page 100.)

ROOTRAINERS Extra-deep modulated seed trays for growing plants like sweet peas from seed. Available online and from garden centres.

SINGLE-DIGGING When you dig a patch of ground to improve the soil texture, remove weeds and get it ready for planting (see page 17 for instructions). You dig to one spade's depth: double-digging is when you dig down two spades' depths (very hard work indeed, so I never do it).

STAKING   When you plonk a pea stick or other support near to a tall or unwieldy plant for it to lean on.

STANDARD   A shrub that has been trained to grow on one stem to a certain height and then allowed to spread out so it looks like a lollipop.

THINNING OUT   Removing some of the seedlings that you've sown in order to give their neighbours room to grow and spread out.

TOP-DRESS   Adding compost or another material, like gravel or leaf-mould, to the surface of the soil in a container.

TOPSOIL   The upper layer of soil on planet earth, which is very fertile and where all the micro-organisms are doing their work.

Little black book

Here are some of my favourite places to shop.

ONE-STOP SHOPS
www.cgf.net, www.clifton.co.uk, www.crocus.co.uk, www.diy.com, www.evergreenext.co.uk, www.gardeningexpress.co.uk, www.homebase.co.uk, www.petershamnurseries.com, www.rassells.com, www.sarahraven.com, www.spinnersgarden.co.uk, www.thegardencentregroup.co.uk, www.wyevale.co.uk

BULBS
www.avonbulbs.com, www.broadleighbulbs.co.uk, www.rassells.com

CYCLAMEN
www.tilebarn-cyclamen.co.uk

FERNS AND IVY
www.fibrex.co.uk

FRUIT
www.blackmoor.co.uk, www.crown-nursery.co.uk, www.otterfarmshop.co.uk

HARDY GERANIUMS
www.plantpref.co.uk

HERBS
www.jekkasherbfarm.co.uk

ROSES
www.classicroses.co.uk, www.davidaustinroses.com

SEEDS
www.dobbies.com, www.realseeds.co.uk, www.secretseeds.com, www.specialplants.net, www.thompson-morgan.com

TOOLS
www.burgonandball.com, www.worldoffelco.co.uk

TWINE
www.nutscene.com

WISTERIA
www.thelaurelsnursery.co.uk

Good reading

I use masses of books for inspiration and advice (too many to mention here but they are listed on my website, www.laetitiamaklouf.com). The books below are my favourites for choosing plants and general gardening counsel.

Choosing plants for your garden: books for list-making
Perfect Plant Perfect Place by Roy Lancaster (Dorling Kindersley, 2010)
RHS Encyclopedia of Plants and Flowers by Christopher Brickell (Dorling Kindersley, 2010)
RHS Plants for Places (Dorling Kindersley, 2011)
RHS What Plant When (Dorling Kindersley, 2011)
Right Plant Right Place by Nicola Ferguson and Frederick McGourty (Cassell Illustrated, 2005)

Practical
Grow your Own Vegetables by Joy Larkcom (Frances Lincoln, 2002)
Hillier Manual of Trees and Shrubs by Hillier Nurseries (David and Charles, 2007)
Jekka's Complete Herb Book by Jekka McVicar (Kyle Cathie, 2009)
RHS Plant Finder (Dorling Kindersley, annual publication)
RHS Propagating Plants by Alan Toogood (Dorling Kindersley, 2006)
The Complete Supergardener by Alan Titchmarsh (Cassell, 2000)
The Well-Tended Perennial Garden by Tracy di Sabato-Aust (Timber Press, 2006)
The River Cottage Veg Patch Handbook by Mark Diacono (Bloomsbury, 2009)

There are thousands of keen gardeners, from first-timers to seasoned professionals who are blogging about gardens and plants. Surfing the web is one way to come across them, or join Twitter where there is a lively community of gardeners who, like me, adore to chat, give advice and answer questions. Find out about all the brilliant people I follow at @LaetitiaMaklouf

Acknowledgements

This book has been 18 months in the making, and so many people have had a hand in bringing it (and the garden on which it depends) to life.

First and foremost, my publishers, Bloomsbury, who encourage me and involve me every step of the way. Natalie Hunt is the creative and organisational genius behind pulling it all together, with a peerless eye and gentle honesty and I cannot thank her enough for her patience and focus. Thanks go also to the brilliant Bloomsbury team, including Anya Rosenberg, Ruth Logan, Amanda Shipp, Alice Shortland, Penny Edwards and Jude Drake. And at WME, thanks also to Eugenie Furniss and Claudia Webb for their help and encouragement throughout.

The amazing Jill Mead has again managed to take the perfect photographs. Working with her is like having a friend round for the day – I always love it. And for deeply gorgeous design and making this book sing its own special song, thanks go to the hugely talented Georgia Vaux.

My husband, mother and father, and my brothers who have supported me and stepped in when I needed help (which I did ... lots) – thank you. And Jemima ... well, it's all for you really little one.

A heartfelt mention to all my Twitter friends, who have been 'with me' all the way as I wrote this book. Thank you for being helpful, funny, brilliant and encouraging. It would have been so lonely without you.

Lastly, and once again, a special thank you to Katie Bond at Bloomsbury, without whom I would possibly not be writing at all. She saw me and told me I could do this, and that makes her a life-changing kind of a person ... wow.

INDEX

PAGE NUMBERS IN *ITALIC* REFER TO THE ILLUSTRATIONS